JAPAN

THE ART OF LIVING

A
SOURCEBOOK
OF
JAPANESE
STYLE
FOR
THE
WESTERN
HOME

●

JAPAN
The Art of Living

A
SOURCEBOOK
OF
JAPANESE
STYLE
FOR
THE
WESTERN
HOME

AMY SYLVESTER KATOH
Photographs by SHIN KIMURA

CHARLES E. TUTTLE COMPANY
Rutland, Vermont & Tokyo, Japan

For Yuichi
Mia and Saya
Tai and Toshi,
who make
everything possible

Published by the Charles E. Tuttle Co., Inc,
an imprint of Periplus Editions (HK) Ltd.
with editorial offices at:

RK Building 2nd Floor, 2-13-10
Shimo-Meguro, Meguro-Ku, Tokyo 153 0064;
153 Milk Street, 5th Floor, Boston, MA 02109;
and 5 Little Road, #08-01, Singapore 536983

LCC Card. No. 89-51951
ISBN 0-8048-1611-5 (Hardcover)
ISBN 0-8048-2133-X (Paperback)

First paperback edition, 1999
Fourteenth printing, 1999

Design by Katharine Markulin
Printed in Singapore

Contents

Foreword

Much of Japanese culture is unique. There is, for instance, the daily hot bath. Born in ancient times out of a need for ritual purity, it shocked the first European visitors, who saw it as a hedonistic addiction imperiling the health.

Just as distinctive is the traditional Japanese house. Prehistoric immigrants to Japan brought ancestral memories of the South Pacific and, nothing daunted by three seasons not at all tropical, built open, airy, up-off-the-ground dwellings beautifully suited to their new land's hot and humid summers but less appropriate for its chill winters. No matter, for, as I was tartly informed forty years ago while huddling over a tiny heater in a large room, in the winter one is supposed to be cold.

The traditional Japanese house is itself a work of art, although today few people can construct one or, if they could, would choose to live in it. Notions of creature comfort have changed, and it is not surprising that all through the countryside farm families have abandoned the traditional houses so appealing to our foreign eyes in favor of modern structures we may find uninspired or even ugly. To the families who lived in them it was no contest, and I admit that I would feel as they do. The new houses are functional and comfortable; the old were not, and by today's standards they never were, for all their much-praised shadows.

We are all familiar with the rhapsodies that sensitive critics have lavished on the traditional room and its magical ability to serve for living, dining, and sleeping, while all the time retaining its simple elegance. For some time I have suspected that such praise was based on the observation of rooms that were not lived in: those that the privileged could set aside solely for receiving guests, or those in a fine *ryokan* (inn). I think I have never seen a lived-in room that was not decidedly cluttered, for architecturally the traditional room affords no place for the miscellany one lives with. Commonly there is not even a place to put the tasteful flower arrangement or the thoughtfully chosen *kakemono* (hanging scroll), the *tokonoma* (alcove) being occupied by the television set. (And where else can it go? It would ruin the tatami.)

But my carping is beside the point. The traditional house represents an ideal, and so more than nostalgia sends us back to it for inspiration and renewal. Superbly crafted of fine woods, luminous paper, and sinewy reeds, technologically innovative in its modular design, this house challenges our standards and prods us to raise them.

More than anything else, the traditional house defines the Japanese style as we Westerners prefer to think of it. The Japanese, however, being a practical and resourceful people, do not so limit themselves. They know that there are times when the spirit breaks the bounds of quiet simplicity, and so they have created Nikko as well as Ise, and love them both. They know that sometimes a theatrical splash is called for.

I cannot elucidate the ineffable something called "style." But I know that it does not constrict, it releases. By setting boundaries it offers freedom.

That is the spirit that enlivens Amy Katoh's piquant shop Blue & White, and it is the spirit that pervades the words and photographs of this book. It opens windows to fresh sensations and new delights.

—OLIVER STATLER

Introduction

The art of living—does such a thing exist in the crowded, noisy jangle of urban Japan? Is it alive even in rural Japan, where ugly power lines stretch over rice fields and rows of dried persimmons dangle not from the eaves of traditional thatch but from corrugated-iron rooftops? Oliver Statler, eminent author and longtime observer of Japan, wonders if such a thing as a beautiful room exists in today's Japan. Unfortunately his doubt is legitimate in some respects. Although the Japanese aesthetic influences designers everywhere and the ideal of the elegantly simple, all-purpose Japanese room inspires many, the sad fact is that the lack of space and what Mr. Statler has called the "litter of living"—throw rugs, television sets, and vacuum cleaners—do not allow all rooms to be beautiful.

Visitors come to Japan with certain expectations. They expect to find the Japan of myth and movie, where people dressed in kimono live in perfectly appointed tatami rooms in quaint and lovely towns. They assume they will find thatched-roof houses, ancient temples, and exquisite modern architecture surrounded by nature perfected, hillsides dotted with green patchwork rice paddies. The truth is that this Japan does not exist, neither in the cacophony of sights and sounds and garish neon of Tokyo streets, nor in the countryside that struggles constantly to emulate Tokyo's glitz.

Japan perfect is a myth. One must, instead, develop a special eye and look for beauty where it is unexpected, where it is not obvious. Call it a "Japan eye," an art of seeing that allows one to sift through the helter-skelter architecture, through the chaos of telephone poles and electric wires, through the frenzy of bicycles, children, and umbrellas to see the beauty and elements of order within. Looking at one's surroundings with a Japan eye means looking past the garish, blue plastic tubs and seeing only the lovely waterlilies that are blooming within. The Japan eye discerns a world of beauty at the concrete police box with its one fresh flower in a

glass jam jar, and at the tiny vegetable shop with its neat tiers of oranges, turnips, and spinach.

This eye for beauty, order, and display observes the inside of the house as well, looking beyond the clutter to the small, budding camellia in the *genkan* (entrance hall); the still life of fruit in the *tokonoma;* the translucent *washi* (handmade paper) stretched over a checkerboard *shōji* (paper-covered, wooden sliding door); the artfully set table awaiting the arrival of a tray of thoughtfully arranged dishes of food, beautiful juxtapositions of shape, color, and texture. The Japan eye is selective and discriminating. It sees the small touches of beauty amid much that is commercial and mass-produced.

This eye delights too in the number of beautiful public spaces evolving from the mingling of influences from East and West in Tokyo and other urban centers. A new design—and a new lifestyle—of beauty and art is blossoming in restaurants, boutiques, galleries, design studios, and "concept buildings" like AXIS in Roppongi and the Spiral building in Aoyama. These public, distinctly Japanese solutions to the challenge of fusing the best of the traditions of the East and the modern technology of the West hold promise of a future when people throughout the world will seek to incorporate the serenity of traditional style into a modern, twenty-first-century world thirsty for warmth and beauty.

Living with a sense of Japanese style and design in a modern household involves breaking rules: living with panache. Let's call it *Japanache,* a new kind of international style. What is *Japanache?* It is the flair for living anywhere today and distilling the essence of Japanese design and spirit from the past. Making the traditional come alive in a modern context requires panache. It entails the unlocking of the mind and the eye. No longer is there just one way of doing or seeing things. The aim is to try all the possible ways of using things, doing things, creating new combinations.

I vividly remember years ago inviting my Anglophile but

traditional Japanese father-in-law for afternoon tea. I was a young bride, and had starched the best linen and polished the silverware in anticipation of his visit. I had baked special cakes and cookies in his honor, but horrified him by presenting them on a latticed bamboo tray. "Oh, no, Amy," he exclaimed in horror at my ignorance. "That tray is not for cookies!" As continental and cosmopolitan as he was, for him the tray I had used was made for one purpose only, the serving of *soba* (buckwheat noodles), and could not be used otherwise! That day I was taught an important lesson about the relationship of form and function in Japan: there are rules about using certain things for certain functions, and I should try to know and respect them. But as a foreigner, I was not restricted by the boundaries of "one form, one purpose" thinking. I was free to use a bamboo noodle tray as I saw fit, just as today I enjoy filling a straw backpack that may once have carried firewood or vegetables with masses of flowers, or lining up old blue and white porcelain saké-cup rests and putting new white candles in them.

By all means, experiment. Surprise yourself (and my father-in-law!). Take these antiques and traditional crafts, textiles, kites, and flowers—the bits and pieces of beautiful Japan that you have discovered—and put them to new and different uses. They will come alive with their new role in life.

In more than three hundred beautiful photographs, we take you into the homes of Japanese and Westerners who have brought Japanese art, antiques, and, most of all, the spirit of Japanese aesthetics to their best-loved spaces—their tables, rooms, entrance ways, walls. We offer these lovely examples of the Japanese art of living as a new source of ideas for inspiration and emulation.

Instill your house with a Japanese sensibility. All it takes is some imagination and a few touches here and there. Experiment, explore, and exaggerate with *Japanache!*

JAPANESE MARKETS

The markets of Japan are rich in people and products. Among those worth visiting are Tsukiji in Tokyo for fish; the morning market in Wajima for seafood and local produce; Nishiki Kōji in Kyoto for food of all sorts; Tōji and Kitano in Kyoto for everything from antiques to octopus; and the farmers' market in Takayama.

Deep appreciation to the generous people who opened their doors
to our camera to give definition to *JAPAN The Art of Living*

Mr. and Mrs. James Adachi, Mr. and Mrs. John Alkire, Mr. and Mrs. Hassan
Askari, Mr. and Mrs. Rex Bennett, Mr. A. B. Clarke, Mr. and Mrs. Carlo Colombo,
Madame Nicole Depeyre, Mr. and Mrs. Matthew Forrest, Mr. and Mrs. Jean-
Claude Froidevaux, Mr. Ichiro Hattori, Mr. and Mrs. Henk Hocksbergen, Dr. and
Mrs. Peter Huggler, Mr. and Mrs. Hiroyasu Isoda, Mr. and Mrs. Yasuhiko Kida,
Mr. and Mrs. Donald Knode, Mr. John McGee, Ms. Kathryn Milan, Mr. and Mrs.
Takamitsu Mitsui, Dr. and Mrs. Komei Okamoto, Dr. Joseph A. Precker and Mr.
Robert Wilk, Mr. and Mrs. James Russell, Mr. and Mrs. Eric Sackheim, Ms.
Patricia Salmon, Mr. and Mrs. Stephen Stonefield, Mr. and Mrs. John Sullivan,
Mr. and Mrs. Yoshihiro Takishita, Ms. Patricia Waizer

With head bowed low in thanks to

Nasreen Askari, Sumiko Enbutsu, Judith Forrest, Keiko Kimura, Miwako Kimura,
Seong Ja Lee, Kyoko Machida, Katharine Markulin, Nucy Meech, Mitsuko
Minowa, Tadashi Morita, Julia Meech Pekarik, Nancy Ukai Russell, Lea Sneider,
Junko Suzuki, Yukiko Takahashi, Mitsuo Toyoda, Fumi Ukai, and countless other
teachers, counselors, and encouragers whose belief in this project helped make
it happen

Very special thanks to
Harumi Nibe and Patricia Salmon

NOTE: The landscape architecture for John McGee's seventeenth-century Kyoto house, shown on page 6, was done
by Marc Peter Keane.

1

Light and Space

Light and space abound in this restored farmhouse. The high beams are tied with straw rope.

A Japanese room is a composition of line and texture and the play of light therein. Its beauty derives from the effect of its shadows, which suggest light, and its walls, which both delineate and allude to space beyond with windows and other vistas. The silent, the unseen, the unexpressed speaks just as tellingly as the spoken, the visible, the obvious.

The Japanese aesthetic is played in a minor key. The subtle is preferred to the obvious. Light implies the presence of shadows, and it is the shadows that are loved. Unlike Westerners, who worship the sun, the Japanese have moon-viewing parties; they use parasols for protection from the sun.

Traditionally it has been felt that things of beauty are enhanced by shadow and reflection. In *In Praise of Shadows,* Junichirō Tanizaki observed that even for household implements Japanese prefer "colors compounded of darkness," whereas in the West the preference is for the "colors of sunlight." The colors of darkness appeal because of the underlying beauty to be discovered within. How much more beautiful the gold leaf of screens and scrolls, the lustrous depth of lacquer, the handloomed weave of a silk *obi* (kimono sash) when seen by flickering candlelight or the gentle light of an *andon* (paper-covered lamp).

The Japanese approach to light can be seen in the Akari light. Inspired by traditional lanterns covered with *washi,* Isamu Noguchi, himself the product of an East-West marriage, created his first Akari lights in the 1950s. These were simple *washi*-and-bamboo lamps designed to capture and diffuse light softly, gently. Well aware of the warmth and beauty of the *chōchin* (traditional wood-and-paper lantern), Noguchi warned against using bright bulbs within.

Some things are better left suggested, undefined, unclear. The Akari light was designed to provide warmth, shadow, and atmosphere, rather than fluorescent clarity. That these beautiful, handmade lights have remained popular for over thirty years, and

are found in even the most modern interiors (pp. 14, 15, 23, and 41), attests to the wisdom of the traditional approach to lighting, as well as to Noguchi's sensitive fusion of traditional and modern ideas.

Shōji and *sudare* (reed or bamboo blinds) create a sensuous, textural atmosphere in a room. The harsh light of day is refined and diffused. The world outside takes on a surreal quality when filtered through bamboo or paper (pp. 32, 34, and 35). Inside, an ordinary room can be transformed into a magical place by *shōji* and *sudare,* which give play to light and shadow.

Shōji help define space too. Closed, they create a wall, a barrier, even a room. Opened, the wall or room disappears. Different types of screens can also be used, from the simple *tsuitate* (free-standing screen) covered with a Clifton Karhu woodblock print in John McGee's formal entrance (p. 39), to the elegant Kanō school screen in the Mitsui house (p. 40). *Fusuma* (sliding doors) also create space, bringing tremendous flexibility to the Japanese interior. Four small rooms circumscribed by *fusuma* can suddenly become one large room. The marvelous flexibility of space created by *shōji* and *fusuma* brings exciting possibilities to modern living, where space is limited. In our own modern apartment, sets of *shōji* on two walls close to create an instant dining room when we entertain guests.

The concept that space is containable even by paper walls is striking to Westerners, who know walls only as solid barriers. Walls, even paper walls, can be effective in maintaining privacy, creating a mood or an instant room. The magic of *shōji!* The power of paper walls!

GENKAN: THE FACE OF A HOME

The *genkan* is the index of the lifestyle inside the home. More than just a beautiful entrance, it is a space for a psychological transition from the public outer world to the private inner world. Visitors are welcomed by a perfect objet d'art, an arrangement of fresh flowers, or a jaunty collection of objects that defines the taste, interests, and style of those who live within.

Above: In the entrance of the Knode home, a collection of hats rests atop a large mizuya (kitchen chest).

Left: Beckoning cats, threatening demons, and menacing masks surprise visitors coming to the apartment of woodblock artist Yasuhiko Kida.

Right: Awaiting Kida-san's departure are beautiful handmade geta (wooden clogs) in an antique Spanish cupboard.

19

IDEAS FOR ENTRANCEWAYS

The entrance sets the mood for the entire house. An unusual painting, a soft light, or fresh flowers can make a statement that is strong or subtle. Doorways can be accented with *noren* (doorway curtains), usually hung at shop entrances.

Right: An eight-panel, linen noren *with a rabbit design welcomes guests and family to the living room of a restored farmhouse.*

Below left: A still life of brown-lacquer boxes and orange gourds on a marble table creates a thoughtful mood.

Below right: A smart silk shade on a bamboo lamp casts a warm

glow over a hat and partially illuminates a bouquet of poppies on the right and a scroll behind.

Right: Guarding the entrance of this restored Karuizawa farmhouse is a bold brush-stroke daruma (representation of the Indian priest Bodhidharma, invoked for his ability to fulfill wishes). The handmade washi paper on which it is painted blocks drafts in the old wooden house. A colorful turtle-and-crane tsutsugaki (free-hand, paste-resist technique of dyeing cloth) quilt cover hangs from the beams over a basket of wildflowers. The flowers are flanked by two small, stone wild boars, symbols of courage and strength. Objects with good-luck motifs are favorite choices for entrances to homes.

AIR AND SPACE

The interplay of paper and light can create different moods, dynamic or restful. Combinations of light, space, and art create different effects.

Above: There is a feeling of airiness in this living room, where paper blinds made of joined squares of crumpled washi *diffuse light without restricting the space.*

Right: A modern genkan *serves as a minigallery for the huge, explosive calligraphy* Kumo, *by Junko Suzuki. Skylights and clean white walls add a contemporary feeling of airiness and space. A* tsutsugaki *quilt cover with a crane motif and a lacquered toy horse from an Aizu Wakamatsu samurai house surround a backpack basket bursting with flowers arranged by Harumi Nibe.*

ANTIQUE TRIO

The use of antiques creates an atmosphere of calm and good taste.

Above left: A handsome nineteenth-century kyokuroku (priest's chair), a scroll with tasseled weights, and a polychrome Imari platter set the mood at the entrance to the Knode house.

Above right: Announcing the arrival of autumn, an arresting flower arrangement in the genkan brings nature inside the house. The charming asymmetry of a Bizen pot from the Momoyama period completes the tableau.

Right: High-tech magic. Hidden behind the warm, wooden craftsmanship of classical Japan is the high-tech craftsmanship of today. Utterly opposing media show the same high level of workmanship and an ingenious use of materials.

GRACEFUL LIVING

Right: The built-in daybed is wrapped in windows. While reading a book or taking a nap you can enjoy the beautiful continuity of the trees outside and the art inside, the carved ranma *(wooden transom)* above and the painted fusuma *to one side.*

Below: Unfinished beams bound with rough rice straw hold the house together, while making a beautiful composition.

INSIDE AND OUTSIDE

Overleaf: The graceful harmony of beauty inside and outside creates an ambience of peace and visual richness. The magnificent daimyō hibachi *(brazier made for a feudal lord)* by the window is framed by two shokudai *(candle-stands)*, creating a spot for conversing and enjoying the Knode garden through the elegant filter of tasseled bamboo sudare.

BAMBOOZLED

One never tires of looking at bamboo, its many forms, its many uses.

Above: Bamboo is silhouetted on the shōji *behind a Bunraku (Japanese puppetry) lectern.*

Left: A yukitsuri *(skirt of straw rope and bamboo) protects trees from snow and wind.*

Right: A bamboo ladle rests on a stone basin.

Below left: Money is said to multiply when washed in the waters of the Zeni Arai Benten shrine in Kamakura.

Below right: An old man of the Meiji era straightens bamboo joints by moistening them, then holding them over fire.

Opposite: A bamboo grove at dusk is an unforgettable memory.

WINDOWS AND LIGHT

Left: In Patricia Salmon's elegant city flat, windows give onto the greenery of a temple next door, providing a natural spotlight for the dramatic sculpture by Masayuki Nagare and light for peaceful reading. Converted bronze shokudai *from the Meiji era make stately lamps. A footed, lacquer tray holds magazines.*

Above: The shape and placement of a window can determine the character of a room. This area was a dark space until the window was added, creating an interplay of light and shadow. Clean white walls and tatami floors contrast with the earthy textures of the beams and reeds on the ceiling.

WINDOW ART

Above: The magic of shōji transforms the bamboo grove outside into alternating patterns of light and dark, nature and geometry.

Left: Kyoto carpenters used masterful techniques to design this bell-shaped, lacquered window. Adjacent is the family altar, originally built in Kyoto and moved to Tokyo some thirty years ago by the Mitsui family.

Right: The historic Sengakuji temple is the famous site of the mass suicide of forty-seven ronin (masterless samurai) in 1703. The marvelous architectural concept of shakkei (use of nearby scenery as a background) blends the temple and its flowering cherry tree with the state-of-the-art architecture of Edward Suzuki. Ascending the stairs of the house of Hilary and Carlo Colombo, one realizes the house was planned around this moment, when inside and outside combine in the meeting of the temple's cherry blossoms and the arrangement of blue and white Imari ware on a tansu (wooden chest).

THE ART OF WINDOWS

The concept of *oku* (distance) is central to Japanese architecture. It serves to lead the eye from the surface to beyond and within. This creates a feeling of space and dimension in a seemingly natural way, though it is, of course, entirely contrived.

Above: The ultimate art is nature, here filtered through reed *sudare* with classic hooks and tassels.

Right: Light creates a perfect space. Details like a copper basin, masterly woodwork, and light represent the thoughtful taste for beauty even in utilitarian places.

Left: *Scores of* torii *(Shinto-shrine archways) dramatically compel the eye and spirit to travel through them to the deities of Zeni Arai Benten, the famed money-washing shrine in Kamakura.*

Right: *The interior serves as a frame for the beauty of nature outside.*

Center: *The carpenter shapes nature. He plans and designs* shōji *that highlight nature's beauty with dramatic, one-of-a-kind frames.*

Below: *Carpenter and gardener join to enhance nature by showing it through a window. By having the outdoors as one of its integral parts, the house itself becomes more beautiful.*

Overleaf: *Soft light filtered through modern* washi *blinds by Hiroshi Morishima gives a shimmering loveliness to the living room of Stephen and Elizabeth Stonefield. The large ceramic rabbit on the coffee table started life as a nineteenth-century incense burner, used to repel insects when kimono were aired.*

LIGHT AND SHADOW

In praise of shadows. Soft, diffused light creates shadows, warm and mysterious.

Left: A lamp on a table with bowed legs lights up the European-style living room. Behind are a classic Japanese wing and garden.

Opposite, top left: A standing Akari light casts a soft glow on a tansu and fish sculpture.

Top right: An oversized fan made of washi and bamboo welcomes visitors with its atmospheric light.

Center left: Used only three or four times in its entire three-hundred-year history, this entrance to a traditional Japanese house was built to welcome an exalted teacher or lord. The series of glowing lights leads the eye to an inner room graced by a tsuitate mounted with a Clifton Karhu woodblock print.

Center right: Andon are ingenious wood-and-paper creations originally designed for candlelight. Construction of the portable lamps varied, depending on how the candle or oil plate was fixed. Repapering the lanterns with old washi or woodblock prints produces interesting effects.

Below left: In the artful corner of kitchen central, an old porcelain saké keg sheds light on note pads used for planning the day's activities. Okame-san (round-faced, smiling woman, the ideal of feminine good nature) gives her silent blessing.

Below center: At the entrance of A.B. Clarke's house, an unusually shaped kabekake andon (bamboo and washi wall lamp) sends a mellow glow over a basket of flowers and a chō dansu (shopkeeper's chest for accounting), a mark of status during the Edo period.

Below right: A wide-brimmed shade over a converted blue and white vase provides light and atmosphere at the same time.

Above: In this aristocratic entrance, the diffused light picks up subtle gold highlights in the elegant screen within and invites you to venture inside.

Far left: An early Showa-era ceiling light casts a glow over a "demon queller" scroll and other paintings, making the staircase a fascinating place to linger.

Left: A reading andon sheds a soft light on its surroundings.

Opposite: Far from wasting space, stairs can celebrate space, as shown here in the Hoksbergen house. Baskets on stair rungs are both handy and attractive. Baskets on the landing add interest too. The large one boasts a huge collection of corks from wine bottles. The simple washi lantern gently illuminates the soft blues, whites, and pinks of the tsutsugaki quilt cover, which bears the auspicious motifs of crane and turtle, bamboo, pine, and plum.

MARRIAGE OF LIGHT AND SPACE

Opposite: The gentle glow of an andon *sends light in different directions, illuminating a nineteenth-century* naga dansu *(long, top-opening chest), a frolicking rabbit* tsutsugaki *quilt cover, and massive beams overhead. Willow branches studded with pink and white rice balls are decorations for the new year.*

Above left: A multifaceted, nineteenth-century andon *stands over a carved wooden cat.*

Above right: Suspended on an old piece of bamboo, a stencil-dyed, indigo yogi (padded sleeping kimono) hangs ready for use during cold Karuizawa winters.

Right: An auspicious Mt. Fuji-shaped candelabrum, probably from a shrine, sits on a disguised heater. Beside it is a hexagonal andon *with an arm to raise or lower the candles for lighting. At night, the flickering candles transform the room.*

2

Traditional Furniture

The beauty of traditional furniture is enhanced when used in dramatic new ways. Here, a pair of Rinpa screens provides the background for two carved fish swimming in the glossy surface of a *tansu.*

The Japanese lifestyle has traditionally been one without furniture, in the Western sense. The outsider is surprised to find in the pure Japanese room nothing more than some floor cushions and an occasional chest. What furniture there is is generally low, angular, and architectural, rather than curved, upholstered, and scaled to the human body.

The traditional appreciation of the functional and the natural has resulted in simplicity, honest workmanship, and sensitive use of materials. Originality and craftsmanship in furnishings like *noren, fusuma, sudare, kakejiku* (hanging scrolls), and *byōbu* (folding screens) have added depth and variety. Both furniture and artwork have historically been linear and asymmetrical, with texture, finish, and natural elements emphasized. The beauty of these elements makes Japanese furniture well suited to modern interiors. The understatement and simplicity of design add dignity and grace to rooms, making clean and unique statements of taste.

Traditional furniture design was strongly influenced by architectural considerations. Architecture was basically in harmony with the natural environment. Inside and outside were joined by architectural elements that defined space. The *shōji, ranma, fusuma, andon,* and *tokonoma* were made of natural materials: wood, bamboo, paper. Carpenters with an intuitive grasp of proportion infused a feeling of warmth and beauty into these otherwise inanimate objects, giving them a strong appeal that transcends time.

Originally purely utilitarian, furniture developed from storage boxes. Merchants and farmers grew more prosperous during the Edo period (1603–1868), and by the beginning of the nineteenth century demand for real furniture had increased considerably. No longer would traditional storage boxes suffice. Instead, specialized chests called *tansu* were crafted according to their function: handsome, massive *mizuya* (kitchen chests); charming,

multidrawered *kusuri dansu* (medicine chests); *fude dansu* (writing chests), with their distinctive inkstones and brush-stained drawers; *funa dansu* (sea chests), heavily weighted to keep from rolling on the high seas; and durable *zeni bako* (money boxes), which have a telltale, round hole for coins at the top, usually with handsome, ironwork reinforcement. All were made by highly skilled craftsmen for specific uses: handsome solutions to practical needs. Their utilitarian nature gives them great charm, as does the lustrous patina they have acquired over the years, and they are highly sought by antique lovers today.

Elegant testimonials to the skills and materials of unknown craftsmen of the past, these traditional pieces of furniture bring dignity and meaning to their surroundings. At the same time the pieces themselves are reborn when used in new and unusual juxtapositions with contemporary furniture.

IN THE TANSU MOOD

Tansu come in all shapes and sizes. The distinctive combination of black ironwork and richly grained wood is persuasive testimony to the craftsmanship of traditional Japan.

Opposite: A Mikuni bō dansu *(chest with a wooden locking bar from the Mikuni region of Fukui Prefecture) draped with an obi is the handsome stage for a lacquered, footed tray from Patricia Salmon's collection. Kumquat branches in an upended pot are playfully repeated in the birdcage above.*

Above left: Atop a kuruma dansu *a stone Jizō (god of children and travelers) and a basket of flowers welcome visitors.*

Above right: The Chinese character for tsu-tsumu *(to wrap) on a straw saké-keg cover hangs behind a fine antique* kannon biraki *(front-opening, double-doored chest) in the Forrest entrance hall, creating a mingei (folk art) mood.*

Left: A standing lamp casts a warm glow on a kannon biraki *chest and a display of primitive sculpture from the Sackheim collection.*

49

PERIOD LIVING

Left: *Over a resplendent* tansu *in the* tokonoma *of Kathryn Milan's Taisho-era Roppongi home and gallery, a charming carved tiger skulks through bamboo. The tiger basks in the glow that also highlights wildflowers in a sculptural bamboo basket and the gilt edges of a black-lacquer stand for an antique Imari plate.*

Below left: *Conversion tables. The large table, a former Chinese door, the small one, a Japanese kimono tray, become mother-and-child, black-lacquer tables holding magazines and fruit, while reflecting the graceful architectural details of Don and Barbara Knode's tearoom, which serves both family and guests alike.*

Below right: *Beautiful corners. The handsome vaulted* Yahata dansu *(chest with distinctive metalwork from Sado Island) with identical stacking pieces sits on a Japanese cotton* dantsū *(carpet).*

Above: Yasuhiko Kida has missed no detail and spared no effort in creating this charming tableau, from the kaidan dansu (step chest) leading to the upper floor storage space, to the traditional hearth sitting area in the middle of neat, square, unbordered tatami mats. The kuruma dansu in front of the shōji was built on wheels to allow for rapid removal in the fire-plagued nineteenth century. A massive, wooden hook hangs over the hearth while a stolid, stone cat stands watch.

51

THE TANSU AT WORK

Opposite, above left: A magnificent wheeled tansu *in the Okamoto entrance provides storage space and supports a stone* koma inu *(mythological animal that is part dog and part lion) from Kyushu.*

Opposite, above right: Another *style of* kuruma dansu *stores linens, place mats, and serving things.*

Opposite, below: A charmingly *steep step* tansu *is dressed up with an elegant* obi.

Left: This kaidan dansu *provides an interesting focal point for a conversation corner of the living room.*

Below left: A kaidan dansu *spotlights the beauty of what it displays.*

Below right: Underneath is a *wealth of storage space for CDs, books, even liquor.*

FIRESIDE CHATS

The *hibachi* was originally a brazier that burned charcoal for heating and cooking. Traditional examples come in all shapes, sizes, and materials, from rattan to wood to the well-loved blue and white ceramic version. Part of their beauty today derives from the multiplicity of ways, both traditional and innovative, in which they can be used.

Above: The Okamotos heat their living room by burning charcoal in their rare, wide-lipped hibachi. *Harumi Nibe's exciting arrangement of white flowers echoes the dynamism of the six-paneled, ''collection of treasures'' tsutsugaki quilt cover used to create this unique couch.*

Right: This copper-lined hibachi *serves as a coffee table, useful for holding magazines, flowers, and drinks. The lovely, antique kimono quilt by Reiko Shishikura titled* Dawn *on the sofa adds warmth and color to the scene.*

Opposite: A graceful blue and white Imari phoenix hibachi *reflects sunshine filtered through* sudare *and serves as a stand for a basket of lovely fall flowers and a carved wooden* daruma.

BAMBOO WORK OF ART

Opposite: Reflective glass supported by an intricately joined bamboo base forms a simple and exquisite table designed and constructed by A.B. Clarke for his light and airy dining room. A masterful restorer of antiques, he combines the best of modern and antique elements and delights in the functionality of both.

Left: This nineteenth-century kuruma nagamochi *(wheeled oblong chest that opens from the top)*, originally used for storing bedding and kimono, serves as an elegant storage space in the Clarke house.

Below: Square bamboo is created by trussing young bamboo to suppress its roundness. The perfection of detail and honesty of workmanship are the fruit of long hours of work by a resourceful American inspired by Japanese craftsmanship.

CLASSICAL ELEGANCE

Right: A Chinese kang is fitted with brocade bolsters and throw cushions made from Japanese kimono and bordered with a narrow gold obi. Behind is a Muromachi-period "Hills of Kyoto" screen. The screen is set on a specially built raised platform and lit to bring out the gold misting. On the floor is an indigo saddlebag carpet from China.

Left: An old kura (storehouse) door cleaned and polished is born again as a spacious writing desk. Wheels on the legs allow for easy movement. A modern Chinese tortoise-shell-bamboo chair is covered with old indigo egasuri (pictorial ikat).

Above: An antique Korean bean chest comes to life as the setting for a handsome collection of nineteenth-century kiseru (smoking pipes). These rich wooden chests come in three sizes. The largest was used for rice, this size was for beans, while the smallest held sesame seeds.

3

Table Settings

Of all the rooms I have seen, this one is unforgettable. Hidden behind ornate Balinese doors, the room is a complete surprise, with its combination of blue walls and *shōji,* Ching and Imari plates, Renaissance drawings and Japanese art.

The table is the heart of the home in any culture. Here families unite to eat, drink, discuss, plan, philosophize, and celebrate. Guests, visitors, and friends are entertained at the table, the inner sanctum of family life. For birthdays, anniversaries, and parties, the table is dressed with elegance. For a simple breakfast, lunch, or tea, it is informal. The table serves, more than any other place, as the scene of daily meals, the setting of special occasions, the seat of family activity.

The Japanese presentation of food is first and foremost visual. Food is often presented architecturally, everything linear and angular around the softness and curves of the artistically arranged food. Dishes of clean blue and white Imari, black-lacquer boxes and bowls, and rough pottery are used as frames to enhance the food they serve. Food too is chosen for its variety of color and texture. The guest delights in the thoughtful presentation that appeals on every level: visual, intellectual, emotional, and, perhaps lastly, gustatorial.

The harmony of food and dish is of special importance in Japanese cuisine. Food is eaten in season, and dishes are chosen to highlight the nature and color of the food. Potter, cook, and farmer work together to create a perfect tableau that captures the essence of food and container. *Okyakusama* (the honored guest) is given all due respect and special treatment. No pains are spared for the visitor. I sometimes suspect that is why Japanese are loathe to entertain at home. They worry perhaps that their home is not elegant enough for a guest, or that they cannot present a table that is special enough. Indeed the standard is frighteningly high!

The concept of *hatsumono* (first fish, fruit, or vegetable of the season) is a key to the Japanese attitude toward food. The first strawberry of the season, the first bamboo shoot, and the tea from the first harvest are anticipated with the same joy as is Beaujolais Nouveau. Host and hostess take great pride in presenting *hatsumono* to guest and family alike.

Setting the table with **Japanache,** however, requires more bravado than perfection of containers and food. It calls for an imaginative combining of layers, of contrasting shapes, colors, patterns, and silverware (or chopsticks and their rests), napkins, tablecloths, place mats, or even trays to highlight the season or occasion.

Japanese elements can bring special dash to the table setting: the gold weave of the *obi* laid down the center of the table reflects the flickering candlelight, the straw basket cradles the flowers and gives them focus. Lacquer boxes and trays frame the food and give drama to even simple fare. Above all, small, delicate portions, artfully arranged with an eye for color and shape, provide visual excitement.

Traditional Japanese wisdom dictated the serving of eight colors during a meal, thirty kinds of food during the day, to ensure a well-balanced diet. While those requirements are impractical today, arranging food, tableware, textiles, and flowers in artistic combinations is an inspiring goal for modern living.

DINING WITH ART

Left: A joy forever is the beautifully constructed two-hundred-year-old Gifu farmhouse of Yoshihiro Takishita. The architecture is simple, massive, and amazingly modern. Here a storehouse door has been put to new use as a dining-room table. Strips of ikat with a galloping-horse motif are stretched over the table, making perfect place settings for four. A rare, nineteenth-century, red-lacquer kyokuroku has been placed at the head of the table. Behind the table is a "thirty six poets" screen portraying five slightly unruly attendants surrounded by poems written in graceful calligraphy. In former days composing poetry was one of the four pastimes of the aristocracy and therefore a popular subject for screens.

Above: A napkin fans out over a blue and white covered bowl and serving plate, creating a contrasting pattern. The deliberate contrasting of shapes, sizes, and colors on a Japanese table is a pleasure for host and guest alike.

STILL-LIFE TABLEAU

Right: Thick sashiko (quilted material) doubles as a playful place setting for Tiffany bamboo silverware and earthenware plates from Mashiko, a pottery center in Tochigi Prefecture.

Left: A bamboo noodle tray is given a new role serving milk and sugar for tea.

Below: A round, red-lacquer platter frames pears and grapes.

68

Right: Circles and squares contrast, making a stunning composition in form and color.

Below: Floating in space is a modern glass table set for four with candles wrapped in washi and simple azaleas arranged in a lovely old basket rescued from the trash. The table, the ko dansu (small chest) in the corner, and the calligraphy scroll on the wall create a marvelous blend of modern and antique, the priceless and the worthless. Truly one person's trash is another one's treasure.

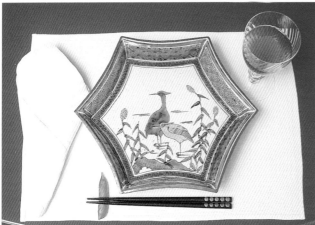

Above: Cooking at the table. In a cozy corner of a Japanese room, a table is set for a winter nabe-mono, *the wonderful one-pot cuisine that is delicious, simple, and enjoyable for all.*

Left: A simple linen place mat and wine goblet give a European touch to the hexagonal Kutani plate.

Right: A splendid, red-lacquer Italian table shows Japanese influence in itself and in its arrangement. Sturdy Kutani plates on fine linen place mats with peapods as chopstick rests are arranged around two large washi cranes. The table is lit by andon and graced by a Tibetan mandala painting in the background.

SURPRISE!

Right: Bob Wilk and Dr. Joseph Precker often entertain in their lovely house. Behind elegantly carved, gilt, Balinese temple doors is a work-of-art dining room remodeled from a former maid's room. Masters of the Japanese art of living, Precker and Wilk take justifiable pride in their artistic table presentations.

Below: A symphony of color. Royal blue walls play against celadon soup bowls atop deep blue Ching serving plates. On the side are Imari plates and lavender napkins, in the center mauve cyclamen in a painted Chinese pot. Green candles in hurricane lamps complete the scene. The orchestration shows tremendous care and promises an unforgettable evening.

Above: The striking Buddhist-temple tapestry on the wall of Don and Barbara Knode's dining room is food for thought. Originally bought as an antique by Barbara's uncle seventy years ago, the hanging has a Japanese theme of white herons on a lotus pond executed in a Western embroidery technique, suggesting it was made at the start of the Meiji era when Western influences were strong. The baroque mood is continued in the cleverly folded *obi* centerpiece that wraps and frames the flowers.

Left: Rich red goblets from Okinawa pick up the red in the polychrome Imari serving plates and soup bowls.

73

Above: *Anemones in a goldfish bowl are the focus of an inviting table set by Nancy Ukai Russell. Blue Ching serving plates topped with contrasting blue and white Imari bowls complete the picture.*

Left: *A beautifully arranged tray blends East and West, the elegant and the rustic.*

Right: *An artistic table for two in the gallery-like home of Dr. and Mrs. Komei Okamoto is a treat for the senses. On the eighteenth-century Spanish refectory table, black-lacquer trays frame rare Imari plates that in turn frame the rolls of sushi. The trays are connected by a sheer, linen runner. Camellias arranged in pottery goblets complete the scene.*

MONPE MASTERPIECE

Left: A remarkable quilt by Yasuko Okamoto of Nagoya illustrates 112 kasuri (ikat, or woven pattern achieved by predyeing threads) styles and patterns found in monpe (farm women's work pants). The jeans of Japan, these blue and white ikat pants were traditionally worn by women working in the field. Though they have practically vanished, the memory of their style and variety is beautifully preserved in this quilt. What pizazz it adds to an impromptu lunch served on Jim and Nancy Russell's rooftop terrace.

Below: When the picture taking took longer than expected, Nancy just covered a table with a patched farmer's quilt cover, warmed up some bread and lasagna, and tossed a quick salad to create an artistic meal.

Right: A feast for the eyes is the harmony found in Harumi Nibe's bouquet of pink and red flowers, grown in her own garden in Hachioji, a suburb of Tokyo. Trained in art, Nibe-san started arranging flowers professionally six years ago. The country spontaneity and fresh sense of color found in her massive arrangements set her apart from traditional stark schools of ikebana. Her quick eye for beauty in nature and in mundane things leads her to arrange flowers in old jars and bottles forgotten by others, as well as in fine, old Imari bowls like those on this table. Nibe-san encourages us to feel that even without training we too can create pretty arrangements with the wildflowers and grasses we find by the side of the road. We learn to enrich our lives simply, by using flowers in unexpected ways and places.

Below: The table is set with a blue and white yukata (cotton kimono for summer) tablecloth to accent the mixed media of antique Imari plates on stark, white serving plates. The clouds and waves of the tablecloth reflect the summer mood of the flowers; the gingko leaves promise fall.

BEAUTIFUL TOKYO TABLES

Opposite: The low still-life centerpiece of persimmons and their leaves on black-lacquer footed trays in the home of Jim and Barbara Adachi does not inhibit dinner conversation as flower arrangements can. The elegant mixture of lace place mats, silverware, crystal, and polychrome Imari gives the table a rich aura of elegant originality. The menu is also a mixture of cuisines, with a Japanese kumquat soufflé for dessert.

Above: French and Japanese antiques join to create the artful dining room of Nicole Depeyre. The clever conversion of a latticework door to a dining table gives the room a light and airy focus.

Left: Soup is served in covered Imari bowls on individual lacquer trays.

4

Japanese Textiles

Horses and diamonds in the
graceful living room of Hassan
and Nasreen Askari. The vivid
colors reflect in tiny mirrors in
the textiles, giving a richness
and palpable warmth to the
room, which celebrates the
beauty of the textiles of Japan
and Pakistan.

Textiles are perhaps the greatest treasure in Japan's remarkable, centuries-old tradition of handicrafts. In a country with few natural resources, human resources are valued highly. Japanese techniques of weaving and dyeing, originally borrowed from Korea, China, and other countries, have developed to a level of virtuosity rarely seen elsewhere. Unmatched skills and a refined aesthetic have combined to produce some of Japan's finest treasures. Lower down the handicrafts ladder, simpler folk textiles have a dynamism and spontaneity that are unparalleled.

Since ancient times, textiles have been revered in Japan. According to legend, when the angry sun goddess plunged the world into darkness by hiding in her cave, other divinities enticed her out with dance and blue and white textile banners. From the eighth century, tribute between Japan and her neighbors, Korea and China, was presented in bolts of silk and brocade. Over the centuries, the Japanese treasured and studied those textile offerings, began producing their own, then further refined them. Some of these textile arts have been taken to the very boundaries of possibility. The brocades of Nishijin silk, the gossamer of summer kimono, the sheer *sha* (silk gauze) kimono of Kyoto aristocrats, and today the magical fibers of Machiko Minagawa for Issey Miyake, transcend the usual limits of textiles.

While textiles have traditionally been used for clothing, crossing over and borrowing from the world of fashion provides rich resources for the home interior. *Obi* sashes are long, narrow jewels of color and style. Given new application hanging on the wall, framing the bed, or folded along the length of the table, *obi* are transformed and revitalized.

To some extent, the traditionalist is barred from this kind of experimentation out of respect for the conventional way of using things. But once conventions are dropped, the *obi* can not only be

wrapped around the kimono, but also about a huge basket of spring flowers, or woven and intertwined with *washi* to make an elegant door decoration for Christmas (p. 113). Kimono too are works of art known for their color and design. Away from the human body, they can be hung on a wall (pp. 160–61) or draped over a couch; taken apart, their beautiful silks and linens can be recycled as cushions, place mats, even lampshades.

Folk textiles are the most obvious items that have crossed over from the realm of traditional textiles to the world of interior design. Country quilt covers, both *kasuri* (woven patterns of predyed threads) and *tsutsugaki,* are charming when used as bedspreads (p. 85) or hung on the wall on bamboo stretchers (p. 101). These textiles give drama to a dining room when used on the table or against the wall. They are fresh and unique in themselves, but their effect is heightened by the fact that they have never before been used in such ways. This creative crossing over is a unique and invigorating undertaking. One experiment leads to another, and the result breathes new life and force into both the house and the objects themselves.

Left: Pattern power. The Chinese character for rice on a blue and white furoshiki (wrapping cloth) is dynamic and modern in concept, though the cloth is really an old piece found at a flea market. Chrysanthemum-petal sashiko stitching reinforces ends that were tied together to carry things, probably futon (bedding). Born again as a tablecloth, this lovely textile sets the tone and coordinates the strong patterns of the arrangement of persimmons and dishes.

Above: The spirit of this colorful "collection of treasures" tsutsugaki quilt cover of the Meiji era is remarkably flamboyant and modern. It gives spark and panache to this bedroom in a modern apartment. The color is subsequently picked up by the Chinese lacquer chests and red pillow covers. A Meiji-era woodblock print hangs over the cloth-covered headboard.

Right: Ebony and ivory patterns contrast and repeat in three similar but different kasuri-covered cushions for the piano.

COUNTRY TEXTILES

How amazing is the range of effect and design achieved by country dyers and weavers who worked in basically just two colors, blue and white.

Above: Kasuri *is the technique of weaving together cotton thread that has been predyed according to a design. This pictorial* kasuri *is remarkable for the intricacy of its woven design. Thrown over a modern couch, it becomes modern itself and balances well with the antique* tansu *and a charming collection of saké cups on stacked trays.*

Right: A Boys' Day kimono, featuring a playful design of a carp leaping up a waterfall, celebrates the strength and daring of the boy for whom it was made. Lively and touching, the kimono brings a childish exuberance to the wall where it hangs.

Above: The mélange of contrasting kasuri patterns brightens the sitting area of this restored farmhouse. The cushions can be used as backrests or for sitting on the floor. The designs of the cushion covers, patched together from workmen's jackets, are strong and distinctive.

Overleaf: The strong geometry of the stenciled linen horse wrapping is stunning when the textile is laid down the length of a double kotatsu (foot warmer) table covered with a huge sheet of glass for dining. Tiny, tear-shaped, blue and white medicine vials serve as vases today, perhaps candlesticks tomorrow. The pink napkins contrast with the modern glass bowls on individual black trays.

GREAT EXPECTATIONS

Right: A mobile of pretty origami (folded paper) cranes and a silk haori (kimono jacket), reversed to reveal designs of good fortune, show the creative imagination of a mother awaiting the birth of her first child.

Left: This masterpiece by Yasuko Okamoto is a detailed record of monpe patterns and also a timely observation on a style of life and dress that has all but disappeared. The colorful kasuri quilt is hung from a gardener's ladder on a rooftop in Azabu.

Right: Real kasuri has been used to show variations in patterns, belts, pockets, and the bottoms of pants. Mrs. Okamoto translates her scholarly sketches of country ways into historical quilts.

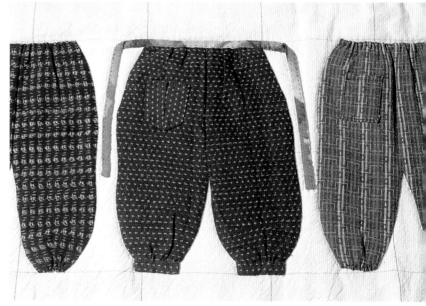

Left: Textile sampler quilts. Carlo and Hilary Colombo's ultra-modern house by architect Edward Suzuki has nice pockets of traditional Japan. A bamboo grove outside is brought inside by the bamboo bench at the foot of the bed. At night, the bench holds the elegant, fan-pattern yukata quilt handstitched by Mary Spellman. An accomplished quilter who preserves historical textiles at George Washington's Mount Vernon, Mary wanted to create something Japanese with yukata materials and her American quilt skills. In this room, antique and contemporary white ceramics contrast subtly with sleek white walls. Korean chests next to the bed hold lamps and a collection of old combs.

Right: Japanese themes and American patchwork patterns make a lovely cross-cultural marriage. The quilted outlines of white cloud patterns give depth to the piece.

Left: Kimono sampler. A variety of kimono weaving and dyeing techniques in a fan quilt inspired by the one above gives quite a different effect in this elegant bedroom, whose mood is echoed in the artwork of Toko Shinoda on the wall. The lovely patchwork by Nobuko Nakata features gentle shadings of color and patterns skillfully contrasted, creating an extraordinary sampler of kimono patterns.

OBI MAGIC, SILK MAGIC

• *Right:* Silk magic. Oshida-san, a mysterious folk god of silk cultivation, has a lustrous, wooden face and a handle hidden beneath a multipaneled skirt of shiny silk and gold brocade. He and a companion goddess (not shown) hang on either side of the doorway to a tatami room in an old farmhouse originally used for cultivating silk. The pair oversees the well-being of the household. The rare figures were probably used in shrines and houses devoted to sericulture.

Above: Obi *magic.* Tansu drawers open to reveal a glorious assortment of brocade obi that Nicole Depeyre has amassed over the years.

Above: A relatively small bedroom with one window inspired Sylvia Sullivan to work her magic using objects at hand. Two obi stretched along the ceiling and draped over a curtain dowel form a regal canopy that is amplified by the graceful lace sheets and plump pillows.

Left: A folded obi lends luster and color to an arrangement of flowers in a Lalique bowl.

Overleaf: Draped dramatically around a wooden dowel hung from a ranma, an obi veils the sleeping space in mystery. With the collection of embroidered silk cushions from China thrown over a bedcover of Japanese brocade, the ambience is both exotic and inviting.

5

Flowers and Seasons

Flowers in their seasons bring
life and vitality to otherwise im-
personal modern interiors and
exteriors. Combining flowers
with unusual containers and
other art elements creates
beautiful moments in time.

No true Japanese home is without flowers. First and foremost, flowers are offered to the gods on family altars where deceased parents and ancestors are remembered. However simple, there is usually some kind of flower arrangement in the *genkan,* where shoes are exchanged for slippers as one steps up to enter the house. In modern apartments, simple yet evocative flower arrangements are displayed in alcoves derived from the classic *tokonoma.*

Flowers bring nature inside the house. They suggest the season or occasion, create a mood both of their own and in harmony with their container. A rough, homely container is often chosen as a counterpoint to perfect, delicate flowers, the flowers appearing more beautiful by the juxtaposition. In fact, the interplay between flowers and container offers endless possibilities for creating a mood. A simple daffodil announces spring, and when the flower is arranged in a fresh cut of bamboo, the newness and wonder of spring enter the room and fill it. Branches of flaming red and yellow maples in a rusty iron pot exaggerate the glory of fall, and at the same time hint at change, at decay, at the end of the harvest. Conversely, there is nothing more joyful than a huge, wooden saké barrel filled with red and white plum branches to announce the long awaited advent of spring.

Flowers are messengers of the seasons. Although they are now available year-round, the plum, bamboo, and pine convey the felicity of the new year. Cherry blossoms can mean only April. In the rainy season of June hydrangea and gardenias bloom. One lovely to see, the other a pleasure to smell, they are a perfect antidote to the daily gray rain.

The concept of changing a house and its decor according to the season is fundamental to Japanese thought. What fun to change curtains to straw blinds, to cover furniture in white linen, to change art to cooler, lighter subjects in summer. Glass plates on the table go

with summery bamboo mats, and a cool, purple clematis floating in an antique goldfish bowl is refreshing in the summer heat.

Seasons mark the celebrations and passages of life. By year's end, all business affairs are completed and debts are cleared, practices harking back to the agrarian tradition of settling accounts when the harvest was finished. The house is thoroughly cleaned and renewed before the new year. New paper is stretched over the *shōji,* new slippers appear at the entrance. As a Western house is decorated for Christmas, the Japanese house is renewed for the new year (pp. 112, 113). Combining elements of both seasonal celebrations is a creative and inventive approach to the art of living with *Japanache.*

Other traditional Japanese customs can lend great joy and color to modern life. Setsubun in February, traditionally celebrated by scattering beans to expel demons and welcome good fortune, is a day the family can enjoy together. The Doll Festival in March brings elaborate arrangements of dolls with their attendant flowers and food, displays that any little girl will love. In May, Boys' Day (now called Children's Day) is a joyful spectacle throughout Japan, where gaily flying carp banners have traditionally been flown from the roofs of homes with boys. Tanabata (the Star Festival) and Obon (the Festival for the Spirits of the Dead) mark the height of summer, when bamboo screens replace curtains and glass wind chimes tinkle in the breeze, the latter an effective psychological cooling system. Changing the interior with the seasons and expressing each season with flowers gives a new and fresh feeling to the house, infusing it with the rhythm of the changes of nature.

Above: White on white. Sensuous shapes of Korean Yi-dynasty porcelain are enhanced by simple white camellias.

Opposite above: Flowers and light. A lacy arrangement of cosmos by Harumi Nibe in a blue and white Imari bowl is gracefully reflected in the inlaid English Victorian table. Candlelight from a washi-covered andon creates a soft atmosphere at night.

Opposite left: Flowers at the entrance give an exuberant welcome and blend nicely with the crane family tsutsugaki quilt cover hanging above.

Opposite right: Saké-keg planter. Even houseplants have Japanache when placed in a saké barrel with decorative straw covering.

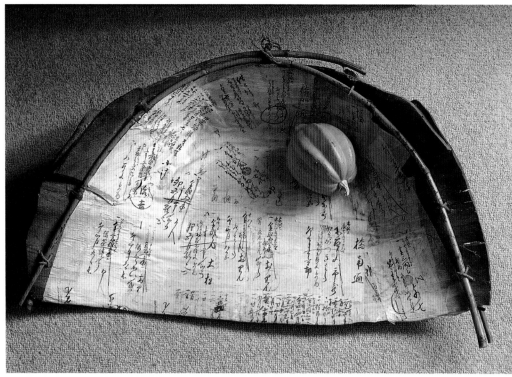

CHECKS AND BALANCE

Just a few simple flowers artfully placed can create a mood or tell a story.

Left: A single gourd in a washi-covered winnower shows quiet beauty and speaks of fall.

Below left: Black and white checkerboard vases frame seasonal arrangements at the Hotel Okura and delight guests and passersby alike.

Below right: Red-lacquer masu (square measuring boxes) filled with water create a checkerboard arrangement of flowers on a modern Italian glass table.

Right: A charming tiger on a blue and white ceramic shard seems to be prancing through an arrangement of crow gourds.

DOORWAY ART

Art and flowers at the door salute guests and passersby and bring pleasure with their unexpected warmth.

Opposite left: A charming antique koma inu *from Kyushu welcomes rather than frightens visitors to the Takishita house.*

Opposite right: Susuki *(pampas grass) means autumn. This arrangement in a bamboo-banded, wooden saké keg is a seasonal greeting from Judy Forrest, whose doorstep arrangements charm visitors and neighbors alike.*

Opposite, below left: Susuki *at the entrance gate of the early seventeenth-century McGee house outside Kyoto is a natural work of art.*

Opposite, below right: The pensive stone deity never ages as he contemplates the changing seasons in the leaves around him.*

HARVEST ARRANGEMENTS: HARVEST BOUNTY

Above: Turtles are thought to live for ten thousand years. This huge turtle, made of rice straw, alludes to the prosperity of a rich harvest. It was made by Toshinaka Yanagida to bring good fortune to all who enter his house.*

Left: Stately autumn maples in Kyoto are filtered through a tasseled bamboo screen.*

FLING OUT THE BANNER

Creating an outdoor flower display requires panache on a large scale. A long banner on a bamboo pole helps frame the creation.

Left: Parts of a display make a display of their own among the bamboo.

Below: Outdoor space is helpful when the elements are large and need to be spread out.

Right: Flapping beside a huge, old rice pot from Kyushu filled with branches of miniature persimmons is an unusual, nineteenth-century Boys' Day banner depicting a colorful procession of humorous, low-ranking samurai. The arrangement of the banner and the persimmons makes an artful entrance worthy of any lordly guest.

ART AND FLOWERS

Opposite: A rainy night dims Tokyo Tower in the background but not the chic of this smart dinner party for four. Atop two contrasting *kasuri* quilt covers, Harumi Nibe has arranged an explosion of summer flowers cut from her own garden and wildflowers taken from the surrounding hills. Using masses of lovely flowers, she brings the very hills where she picked them to the dinner table of this city apartment.

Above left: The seventeenth-century Genji-Heike battle screen contrasts with the pastoral mood of the flowers.

Above right: Even the drawers of a *tansu* can be used as flower containers. In the Askari entrance are sweet bouquets of pink and white clover wrapped in old, block-printed *washi*.

Below left: Madonna with flowers and temple architecture. An unexpected arrangement of wildflowers peeks out from an antique wooden temple post overlooked by Picasso's tender mother and child.

Below right: Flowers in the kitchen. Pink flowers blend nicely with the blue and white Vietnamese canisters and dragonfly tiles handmade by Kaoru Fujisaka. Note the clever system of hanging baskets from bamboo hooks on wooden dowels for easy use.

SEASONS GREETINGS

Above left: Winter camellias from the garden come alive in an old bamboo basket lined with washi. Paper complements flowers and acts as a pretty backdrop.

Above right: Table art. A red and gold obi reflects the Christmas spirit of the flower arrangement by Sylvia Sullivan for Leslie Bennett's festive Christmas buffet.

Above: New Year's decoration. Red and white fans, rice-straw ropes, and folded paper are festive symbols for New Year's, Japan's equivalent to Christmas in the West.

Right: The glittering Precker-Wilk Christmas tree accented by candles is given a Japanese touch by the handsome arrangement of ukiyoe woodblock prints on the wall. Literally "pictures of the floating world," ukiyoe depict everyday life and its pleasures from the seventeenth to the nineteenth centuries.

110

In the seventeenth and eighteenth centuries, sugar, salt, and sesame seeds were treasured commodities. When given as presents, they were wrapped in ceremonial folds of *washi*. These traditional paper folds are the inspiration for the unique miniature sculptures of Ichirō Hattori.

Left: The whimsical Okame-san mask and spray of auspicious bamboo, plum, and pine were made by hand by Hattori-san.

Below left: Miniature miracle. One-of-a-kind masterpiece, an arrangement of ten washi-and-bamboo paper folds based on the traditional folds for gifts of salt, sugar, sesame seeds, and other condiments.

Below right: Hattori-san listens to Italian opera as he works in his workshop. The precision and warmth of his art are unsurpassed.

NEW YEAR'S, JAPANESE STYLE

Everything is made new for the new year. At a time when nature is dormant, people make their own decorations to renew the house and its spirit. Traditional floral decorations are displayed until January 15, Ko Shōgatsu (Little New Year's), when they are taken down and eaten or burned.

Above left: In the Chichibu house of Hiroyasu Isoda, a spray of branches is brought inside and decorated with various auspicious shapes made of sticky rice.

Above right: A long-lived turtle made of rice.

Center: A rice-cake mortar and pestle symbolize plenty.

Below left: Kezuri hana (wood shavings shaped like flowers) are attached to all parts of the house, including the family altar.

Below right: The main porch pillar is decorated with bamboo branches and delicate wood flowers.

Opposite, above left: An elegant arrangement of red paper and mizuhiki (paper cord) wrapped with a festive gold obi makes an original and striking East-West, Christmas-New Year's decoration on the door of John and Sylvia Sullivan's apartment.

Opposite, above right: Straw, paper, pine, and recently plastic New Year's decorations are hung everywhere, including this front door in Asakusa, to renew and beautify one's surroundings.

Opposite, below left: A simple decoration hangs over the noren of a downtown restaurant.

Opposite, below right: Even the hood of a car is adorned for the new year.

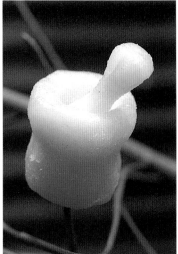

お食事

6

Fine and Folk Art

Bright, lively art comes from the surprising combination of the spare geometry of a brocade *obi* and the sharp eyes of a wide-mouthed *shishi* (mythological creature, half lion and half dog). The arrangement is atop a chest lacquered with the technique known as *negoro* (application of red lacquer over black).

The arts of the emperor, the shogun, and the daimyo have been widely exhibited throughout the world and are well known. The mention of Japanese art conjures up images of Kanō school screens, exquisite lacquer chests, and elaborate Imari bowls. This art—refined, dynamic, and highly sophisticated—was made by master artists and craftsmen under the patronage of the ruling class. The artistic sensibilities of leaders like Oda Nobunaga and Tokugawa Ieyasu, for example, were in strong contrast to their militaristic and often violent natures. Since art was regarded as not only worthwhile in itself but also useful for establishing a patron's status and demonstrating his good taste, elegant arts and crafts were in demand by territorial lords struggling for power and position.

The high standard of art continued through the peaceful and productive years of the Edo, or Tokugawa, period (1603–1868). During this time, a prosperous merchant class evolved, and proved to be a source of new patrons for craftsmen. Art changed as tastes became more popular. With the evolution of the *chōnin* (merchant) culture, the arts of the people bloomed, particularly during the Genroku age (1688–1704). In demand were richly ornamented textiles, lacquerware, and furniture. Money flowed, and arts and crafts became more extravagant as life became more luxurious. Keen competition among artisans and patrons produced spirit, animation, and originality in the decorative arts.

Folk art, on the other hand, comes from the tradition of making things to be used, rather than objects for decoration. Ordinary articles for daily use have long been made by farmers, woodsmen, and fishermen. These simple items were made by hand from available materials: wood, paper, bamboo, straw, and stone. Never frivolous, but often playful, they are made for eating with, for work, for play, even for prayer. Their straightforward honesty gives them universal appeal.

Crafted by unknown hands, much folk art has vague origins. The shape and function of some items, however, provide clues to who made them and for what task. Witness the carpenter's plumbline tool, the fisherman's spiraling iron spear, the woodsman's bucket for gathering lacquer from trees. Baskets too were made for particular uses: strong vine baskets for collecting stones, flat trays for housing silkworms and the mulberry leaves they feed on, and conical baskets with handles for extracting salt from the sea. Function begets form. Form begets beauty.

Materials also hint at the provenance of folk pieces. *Noragi* (work clothes, particularly for farmers) are usually from the cold, northern region of Tohoku, where hemp is cultivated. Beautifully carved, burnished wood pieces often come from the Hida region of Gifu Prefecture, famous for its lumber. Fine bamboo baskets even today are a specialty of Kyushu, where the finest bamboo grows.

In his adaptation of Sōetsu Yanagi's *The Unknown Craftsman,* Bernard Leach calls these utilitarian pieces "effortless products of daily living." Put to use today, they bring a rough-hewn beauty and honesty to interiors, and their humor and very human qualities bring warmth as well.

Left: *A lovely Taisho-era gold screen sits atop a midnineteenth-century* katana dansu *(sword chest). On the tatami in front is a small, lacquer* te aburi *(hand warmer) with cuttings of the season's flowers, wild chrysanthemums.*

Above: *Gold cloud effects were the clever invention of early screen painters who used cloud interruptions to shorten epic stories to fit within the screen. This elegant screen rests on a special shelf and lends its graceful beauty to the dining room of the Adachi apartment.*

119

THE BEAUTY OF USEFUL THINGS

Books as art. Books neatly arranged on bookshelves or on a coffee table are beautiful in themselves and in the worlds of knowledge they contain. Roomy shelves in Stephen and Elizabeth Stonefield's living room keep books visible and readily available. Collections of old books on specialized topics, art books, and novels all have a place on the Stonefields' bookshelves.

Right: Chinese scholar's ladder. A tortoise-shell-bamboo ladder gives access to books on even the highest shelves in the Stonefields' living room. A large sumie (India-ink drawing) calligraphy scroll hangs next to a Korean chest topped with mingei toys. A contemporary basket hanging on the wall is the base for an old basket filled with flowers.

Below: A wooden bucket filled with a charming collection of brushes is characteristic of Elizabeth's humorous and original way of finding beauty in unexpected places.

FLYING DRAGONS

Above: Dragons cavorting about the screen in A.B. Clarke's living room give splash and action to the room. A contrasting red fan is spread over a fireplace when the fireplace is not being used. Note the huge backpack basket filled with greenery hanging on the wall.

Right: An early nineteenth-century screen is decorated with fans in the harimaze (patchwork) style. The paulownia ranma is unusually long and makes a wonderful headboard for a king-size bed. A tall, lacquered basket, once a peddler's chest, serves as a blanket chest in Patricia Salmon's elegant bedroom.

Right: The study of art. Sylvia Sullivan researches a style in her rich, oxblood-colored study. The ceiling moldings have been smartly lined with obi.

Below: An elegant entry. Under an exquisite eighteenth-century screen, an antique bronze gong announces visitors at the Adachi entrance. A fisherman's basket holding yellow leaves from the stately gingko tree outside heralds the season.

Overleaf: Glamorous living in the home of John and Sylvia Sullivan. Sylvia, an interior designer, has adopted the Japanese art of living with flair. A fine Edo-period screen dominates the Texas-size living room, uncommon in Tokyo. The striking collection of sang de boeuf porcelain on the right gives the room a lustrous richness and depth.

123

THE DRAMA OF SCULPTURE

Three-dimensional wooden art was an integral and functional part of the traditional architecture of Japan. Largely made for temples and shrines, it is lively and direct, and adds dimension to modern living.

Below: This carved deity was originally an architectural support in a Japanese temple.

Above left: A Kannon (goddess of mercy) sculpture surveys the surroundings from the balcony of the McGee house. The house was built in the Taisho era with a special balcony overlooking the living room so that the father could view his son's martial-arts training.

Above right: An ancient deity from Nara, carved in the Fujiwara period, is dramatically lit on its piano dais. Mr. McGee regularly rotates pieces in his exceptional collection to achieve different effects.

Above: Primitive sculpture from New Guinea fits in beautifully in Eric Sackheim's rich study. The saké-keg lamp casts a warm light.

Top: A wooden portrait sculpture of a Muromachi-period daimyo seems quite at home against the natural setting of the shōji in the gallery and house of Yoshihiro Takishita.

Left: Artful steps. The step tansu is an effective stage for a collection of sculpture.

Above: This artistic combination features an old banzuke (list ranking sumo wrestlers participating in a tournament), a shishi mask, and a square, blue and white Imari plate, overlooked by Michizane, the scholarly priest.

Overleaf: A Kyoto temple screen is the centerpiece in the Adachi living room. Its elegance sets the tone for a bright, inviting room filled with comfortable furniture and a coffee table piled with the latest books on all subjects: humor, history, art, and culture.

7

Collections

A dramatic collection of Chinese oxblood porcelain on a French buffet commode sets the tone for the whole living room. The effect of arranging the collection en masse is much stronger than placing the pieces separately.

A discerning eye and singular
passion give the collector a unique way of looking at Japan. His
interest may be in smoking pipes, calligraphy brushes, elegant Imari,
or common playing cards, but whatever he collects he interprets
Japan in light of that interest. The world of saké cups becomes a
microcosm of the larger cultural whole. The provenance of the cup,
who made it, why it is as it is becomes a cultural, historical, and
artistic study. The collector delights in this miniature world and
passionately searches for new pieces and new information about
them.

Collecting is a rewarding, if consuming, passion that is
particularly widespread in Japan, where crafts have been refined
and developed over the centuries. Whether it is the idle farmer
carving the simplest *jizai kagi* (hook for hanging a pot over a fire,
p. 51) or the skilled artisan crafting a sophisticated piece of
lacquerware, Japanese hands have rarely been still. They are always
forming something even if it is only a simple folded paper crane. The
collector is the benefactor of this compulsive dexterity, and Japan,
even today, is a paradise for collectors.

Many *tansu* drawers, when opened, allow secret, wonderful
glimpses into the passions of collectors. Museums house the larger,
less secret collections, like the Hatakeyama collection of tea
utensils. The Japan Folk Craft Museum has the rich collection of
Sōetsu Yanagi, the museum's founder and the philosopher behind
the folk-craft movement. The Idemitsu collection of ceramics and
Zen paintings, the kite museum at Nihonbashi, and the paper
museum at Oji are all outstanding testimonies to the single-minded
focus of collecting.

In the extreme, collectors are addicts. They must find that
unusual noodle cup, they must have that bamboo basket, that doll.
Their passion is contagious. Witness the ever-increasing number of
people flocking to the weekly flea markets.

For Westerners and Japanese alike, the flea market is a ready source for building collections. Here, spread out on the mats of the dealers, is the history of Japan of the last fifty to one hundred years. Anyone with some curiosity and a good eye can spot something interesting and start a collection. But the hobby can become an addiction, let me warn you. Once you buy one antique you particularly like, you will find yourself going back again and again, trying to find another treasure. All of a sudden, you are a collector! A good friend, a doll collector, became so absorbed in finding new pieces that she kept going to all the flea markets, each week a bit earlier, trying to get there before other like-minded collectors, many of whom she had educated herself. Long after her husband had declared they had no more room, she was still prowling the markets, still finding more treasures. In doing so, she had unwittingly become an expert on the subject and had a television special focus on her doll collection.

Once your collection is started, the next challenge is to display your treasures effectively. In Japan, where everything is meticulously arranged, display is a fine art. By careful observation, we can all learn some of the many methods of display: simple groupings of like colors and shapes, groupings of contrasts, or groupings of things piled together to delight the observer with sheer abundance (pp. 150, 151). Even unopened boxes (p. 150) arranged together present a feeling of collection. An elegant sensibility can rule over the most mundane grouping of objects, giving them life, and at the same time revealing the focus and passion of the collector.

COLLECTIONS: A CLOSE UP

Left: The eye-catching, fluted blue and white bowl is decorated on three levels. In the center is a crane flying over waves; midlevel are auspicious symbols of pine, bamboo, and plum; outside, rabbits jump through waves. The bowl rests on the grid surface of a thick table used for go (a Japanese board game).

Above left: A tansu treasure. Blue and white and polychrome Imari dishes fill the shelves of the Meiji-era mizuya and make for tempting browsing in Mr. Takishita's sumptuous House of Antiques.

Above right: A kotatsu, the size of one tatami mat, serves as an effective stage for an unusual antique smoking stand, complete with a clock and blue and white porcelain pot for ashes.

Right: A fine eighteenth-century Kanō school painting of snow herons hangs over the fireplace of the Takishita farmhouse. On the right is a nineteenth-century crane tsuitate painting.

ONE MAN'S PLEASURE

Left: Books are one of the many collections of the Sackheim family. Colorful items anywhere, books have a beauty that is comforting and stimulating.

Center left: A wooden sculpture of a Buddha looks down mysteriously from a shelf.

Center right: A favorite piece of Imari sees frequent use as a fruit bowl or serving dish. Using pieces of a collection in daily life keeps them clean and fresh looking. Dust has no time to collect.

Below: Lacquer tsuzura (clothes boxes) are beautiful and practical containers for scarves and stoles. These traditional boxes have been made for hundreds of years for storing kimono and other clothes. How well they are suited to the needs of modern living! They can be specially ordered with family crests from the few craftsmen who fortunately still make them.

STYLE: MODERN AND CLASSIC

Left: A droll series of papier-mâché masks by Toshie Kosuge of Chichibu adds humor to the shōji *where they are hung.*

Center: The unusual mandala of a thunder god hangs behind a sword stand, while below is a selection of water droppers collected by Yasuhiko Kida.

Below: In the smoking corner are various kiseru. *Also shown are pouches and other smoking accessories for the man of the nineteenth century.*

137

HOW TO DISPLAY
A COLLECTION

Collections are simply multiples of objects in one genre. Displayed together, the objects form a pleasing and effective whole. Even small, relatively insignificant things become memorable when displayed as a collection.

Right: Hanafuda *is a card game epitomizing the Japanese approach to play. In ancient times, the Japanese painted pictures on seashells and played games matching them. Three hundred and fifty years ago, the Portuguese introduced cards with numbers. The Japanese accepted the cards but instead of numbers drew pictures of plants and flowers to indicate the twelve months of the year. A set of four slightly different cards represents each month, training the eye to discern subtle artistic distinctions.*

138

Left: Hashioki *(chopstick rests)* are another popular collectible. These singular pieces vary endlessly in size, shape, material, and color. They often have seasonal themes or are amusing replicas of real-life items. Framed in the grid of a kotatsu *table, they make a charming decoration.*

Above: A horizontal shōji *found at a flea market provides an instant frame for a selection of* hanafuda *cards. The cards have been randomly pasted onto the repapered* shōji. *Two antique blue and white Imari* haidai *(saké-cup rests) serve as a base for the* shōji *and* hanafuda.

FASCINATING COLLECTIONS

Left: *With a woodblock-print trip-tych as a background, a small grouping of similar objects becomes a collection. This selection of pottery is displayed in a corner with art objects, books, and flowers in an antique copper saké set used for traveling.*

Center: *On a wall are shelves containing variety and surprise. Combinations of sculpture, ceramics, baskets, and books provide pleasing contrasts of texture and shape.*

Below: *The impact of like colors or shapes arranged in multiples is pleasing and strong, as shown in this kitchen corner.*

Left: The open shelves of an antique Welsh pine cupboard are the setting for this large collection of blue and white Imari soba cups. The cups, in various shapes and patterns, are charming to look at and ready for quick meals at the kitchen counter. Alison Hoksbergen has covered the table with a patchwork quilt she made from men's yukata samples. The quilt blends beautifully with the blue and white plates and cups.

Below: A country cupboard of pine contrasts and at the same time blends beautifully with the softness of old blue and white Imari cups.

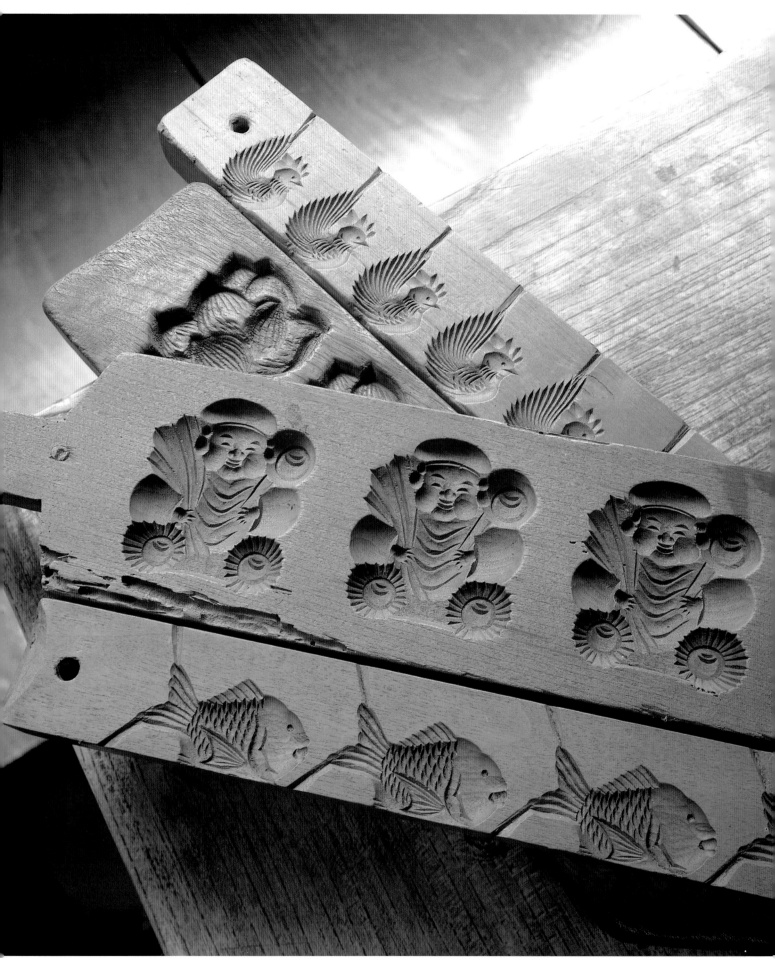

THE ART OF WOODEN CAKE MOLDS

Collected and displayed, even the most mundane objects have great charm. Whether stamps, matchbook covers, or saké bottle labels, there is artistry in the design of each piece and artistry in the arranged collection.

Left: Felicity of pattern and naiveté of design make these traditional cake molds a popular collector's item.

Right: Displayed on the wall, the molds catch light and shadow in the depth of their carvings. Discarded by confectioners when they are no longer usable, the inexpensive molds are still plentiful in antique shops. When hung together on a wall, they form new patterns, many of them light and whimsical. The molds are at once simple and yet very accomplished carvings. On the kura door now used as a table is a square vase with a wave motif by Mia Katoh.

143

DESIGNER KITCHENS

Above: Past and present are combined in a charming kitchen corner. Traditional bamboo baskets find new uses holding fruit and kitchen tools. In front is a jaunty tea cozy made from red and white yukata *cloth.*

Left: The system kitchen, first designed years ago, provides efficient use of space. Today, when space is even more valuable, we can still make good use of the system kitchen. This Taisho-era kitchen boasts a charming, slanted ceiling with bamboo screens, screens over lights, and open shelves for attractive display and instant access.

Below: Behind the scenes is a mixed selection of antique Imari plates and modern Western serving dishes.

Above: Bamboo wall art.

Left: The open shelves of this modernized farmhouse kitchen provide easy access and storage space. Baskets overhead are useful for storing and serving food.

Below left: A former knife basket now bulges with bamboo kitchen utensils.

Below right: This black-lacquer, three-chambered kamado (earthen cooking stove) took care of the needs of a seventeenth-century country household.

A COLLECTOR'S PASSION

Above: Nicole Depeyre, the ultimate collector, was born in Japan and has spent most of her life in Asia. Brought up with antiques and now considered an expert in that field, Madame Depeyre has a fine eye for treasures and is always on the lookout for new and unusual pieces. Her taste is wonderfully eclectic, as shown in her glorious living-room gallery, an opulent composite of Asian art.

Left: A trio of Thai Buddhas overlooks a large living room bursting with items that display her passion for beauty. Note the Cambodian silver at right and the clever use of the hibachi as its stand.

147

ANIMAL ART

When Buddha lay dying, he summoned the animals to bid them farewell. The cow was the first to hasten to the scene but the rat, riding on the cow's back, jumped off and arrived first. Thus the rat became the first animal in the Oriental zodiac, a cycle of twelve years that assigns a different animal to each year. A person is thought to take on characteristics of the animal representing the year in which he or she was born.

Rat: Charming but fussy about small things, thrifty but easily angered.

Cow: Patient and quiet, inspiring confidence in others but eccentric.

Tiger: Strong, sensitive, courageous but stubborn and short-tempered.

Rabbit: Talented and ambitious, virtuous and reserved.

Dragon: Healthy and energetic but excitable and stubborn.

Snake: Deep, quiet, wise, and fortunate in money matters.

Horse: Skillful at compliments, popular, cheerful, and talkative.

Sheep: Elegant, highly accomplished in the arts, passionate but timid.

Monkey: Clever, skillful, original but erratic.

Chicken: Deep, busy, and devoted to work but eccentric.

Dog: Honest and loyal, with a deep sense of duty.

Wild boar: Chivalrous and gallant, with inner strength, fortitude, and honesty.

Above left and right: Wooden fish gongs announced the arrival of visitors to a temple.

Center left and right: Maneki neko *(beckoning cats)* bring prosperity to shops.

Left: This wall, a plaster collage of roof tiles, is in Kyoto's Gion district.

Right: Rabbits and waves were created by Hitoshi Kutsukake, a plaster craftsman in Kyushu.

Opposite: Rabbits everywhere!

Above: This incredible array of tools and art supplies is found in the studio of Yasuhiko Kida. He knows where each one is, and what job each can do. Mr. Kida's wood blocks originate in his keen and humorous observation of the daily lives of ordinary people in and about Kyoto, its markets, temples, and festivals.

Right: Behind the scenes is a storage room filled with pieces of art waiting their turn to be displayed. Storing things is a crucial part of the Japanese gallery-like approach to interior arrangement.

Left: Everything the artist needs for applying color is found here: brushes, paint jars, inkstones. The arrangement of the artist's tools becomes art itself in these orderly displays.

Center: Everywhere you look in the Kida home is a collection. Cutting knives, every kind imaginable, create a wonderful scene of chaotic order.

Below left: These antique dolls are attractively arranged for the Hina Matsuri (Doll Festival) on March 3.

Below right: This sculpted lacquer piece was created by Tatsuaki Kuroda.

8

Beautiful Rooms

An elegant Spanish-influenced house built in the 1930s includes graceful Japanese touches like the moon-viewing window, which looks onto a tatami dining room behind. Bamboo latticework in a round window creates partition while suggesting space.

Walk into a room, any room, and you will meet someone. A distinct personality greets you whether the room is simple or elaborate, a bathroom or a living room. There is a certain aura to the space, as the room takes on, by design or otherwise, the character of those who live there.

Beautiful rooms in Japan, as elsewhere, come about as the result of much thinking, planning, and designing, although the most beautiful rooms are those in which the planning is invisible. Beautiful to the eye, they are also comfortable, encouraging you to relax and feel at ease. Of course, such a combination of graceful beauty and natural practicality, although highly desirable, is not easily achieved.

The classic furnishings of traditional Japan are found in these rooms. The distinctive *tansu* with its striking balance of mellow wood and black ornamental iron, the blue and white porcelain *hibachi,* the basket filled with fresh flowers, and the *washi*-papered *shōji* at the windows—these create an atmosphere of warmth and dignity. When fused with the practical values of comfort and simplicity, the aesthetic values of elegance and creativity add dimension to modern rooms. Seamlessly combined, these values can create some of the most impressive rooms.

Behind every beautiful room is the human desire to live with beauty—in furnishings, in their arrangement, in the light that infuses them, in the art that envelopes them. Beautiful screens, scrolls, paintings, and flowers can all be arranged in a modern Japanese style that is quickly becoming a modern international style.

Part of the appeal of these rooms comes from the fact that they are not just beautiful, but that they are arranged to be livable and useful as well. Graceful step chests (pp. 52, 53) are all-purpose storage spaces, as well as stages for displaying a lovely bowl or a handsome *obi. Hibachi* (pp. 54, 55) become integral parts of daily life, for entertaining guests, for serving drinks, for providing a fresh look for a basket of flowers or antique wooden *daruma* (p. 55).

Traditional pieces come alive when used in refreshing, new ways. Old materials used in new ways can also make rooms beautiful, as shown by the bamboo table on page 56. Beautiful rooms result from the happy combining of old ideas and antiques with new ideas and modern furniture.

This is the ideal. How can we achieve it when we don't have all the classic requirements, the priceless screen or the magnificent *tansu?* By adding a little **Japanache,** that sprinkle of surprise, fun, the unexpected: the birdcage used for a spray of flowers (p. 48) or the patterned inner side of a *haori* draped over a crib (p. 90). This clever use of old things in an original way gives great dash to a style of living. It doesn't take much. Even a few *hanafuda* arranged on a castoff *shōji* (p. 138) can make a corner come alive, can give depth to a room, adding humor and the sense of the unexpected.

ALL LINES CONVERGE

Traditional and modern alike achieve a remarkable dimension of depth and focus, despite different approaches to decoration, one quite stark, the other truly decorative.

Right: Taking the classic precepts of Japanese art and architecture and applying them to modern living requires a certain eye and Japanache. Here the end result is a powerful setting for the magnificent screen. Other elements of the living room, like the handsome Chinese bronzes on the glass table in the foreground, lead to the magic moment when the flapping cranes convene.

Below: A classic model is the traditional tatami room with its lines leading to the tokonoma, where fresh flowers are arranged in a bowl in front of a *sumie* scroll in true Japanese style.

THOUGHTFUL ARRANGEMENT

Above: A stone Jizō sits in front of a fireplace flanked by handsome bronze candlestands. The hibachi in the foreground is a useful table for cups and glasses. The huge, antique teapot surprises visitors as they enter the room.

Left: A shōji window with an outline of Mt. Fuji, bought at an antique shop and installed by Henk and Alison Hoksbergen with the help of a clever carpenter, creates a unique window above a funa dansu in this inviting library.

Left: It is time for a party in this lovely space. Close friends gather for lunch at the Forrests' house to discuss various preservation projects. They are no doubt inspired by the graceful interior, where East meets West.

Right: Lucky guests will enjoy this lovely buffet, graciously arranged on selected serving dishes, a combination of Forrest family pieces and Japanese bowls, antique and contemporary. A kite shows interest from the wall.

Below: In front of a Chinese lacquer screen sits cool white, silk furniture. A simple budding plum branch tells us it is winter and all is distilled to essences.

SILK ROAD RICHES

Right: The striking synthesis of textiles from Pakistan with Japanese kimono and kasuri materials reflects Nasreen Askari's keen eye for texture and color. The rich textiles give warmth and flamboyance to the Askaris' inviting living room. The rare hexagonal keyaki (zelkova wood) hibachi is filled with autumn grasses arranged by Harumi Nibe. On the wall the blue silk kimono with the theme of asobi (play) is a playful counterpart to a Sindhi wedding shawl from southern Pakistan.

DISCOVERED ART

The juxtaposition of serious art and common items from daily life can create lightness and humor in rooms.

Above: Handsome pieces of smoked bamboo have been made into lamps and placed on an ultramodern table made with concrete supports salvaged from a road construction site. Red-lacquer lunch boxes on both sides of a seated Buddha add a pretty accent.

Right: A stone Buddha sits serenely on a kotatsu table. In back is a bamboo basket that Elizabeth Stonefield keeps filled with orchids.

Opposite: A seventeenth-century Genji-Heike battle screen overlooks a living room filled with art and artifacts from all over the world. The carved wooden table, a Spanish antique, contrasts with a homemade table formed by covering a Japanese farmer's basket with a sheet of glass. Two guardian shishi seem to appreciate the humor, and a mirror above doubles the fun.

LOST IN TIMELESS SPACE

Twelve years ago this two-hundred-year-old *gasshō zukuri* (traditional A-frame farmhouse with a steep roof) from Gifu Prefecture was knocked down and transported three hundred miles to the northeast by Yoshihiro Takishita. It took ten carpenters two-and-a-half months to reassemble the six-level puzzle.

Left: Upon entering, one is enveloped in the calm and peace of this room. Furnishings are sparse and utilitarian. The nineteenth-century sleigh has been cushioned in old blue and white cotton *futon* material.

Above: A fireplace has been added in the former entrance. Beams left over from the construction are covered with old rag-weave cushions for fireside chats.

165

Right: An eighteenth-century Venetian settee with curved arms sits beside a modern Chinese bamboo chair. Both lend character to a room that masterfully blends the best of East and West.

Below: A 1950s house built along modern Japanese lines is a perfect setting for European details. The combination of European curves and Japanese angles creates a style that is original and refreshing. The shōji and Japanese art blend well with the European furnishings, notably the unusually large nineteenth-century English butler's table. The combination creates a contemplative mood in the living room of Joe Precker and Bob Wilk.

Above and left: Joe Precker and Bob Wilk spend holidays in Venice, their second home, so it is only natural that they bring some of their European treasures back to their Tokyo house to mix with Japanese art and other Asian antiques. Round-backed European chairs and tables contrast effectively with the square grids of the shōji. Mirrors and glass lamps enlarge the room and multiply its treasures. Hercules, a two-thousand-year-old Roman copy of a Greek original, surveys the East-West blend with pleasure.

A PLACE FOR EVERYTHING

A beautiful room is the sum of its beautiful parts. The thoughtful arrangement of every corner, blending Japanese art and antiques with Western furniture, creates surprise and provides stimulation. The eye delights in the imaginative use of art and antiques in surprising ways. Even mundane objects can become beautiful when used in unexpected combinations.

Above left: A careful arrangement of scrolls and chairs makes a pocket of space where two people can sit and talk about art or anarchy or anything.

Above right: This interesting corner, featuring an unusual stack of boxes topped with a basket of flowers, combines art and utility.

Above: Even an unwanted column is useful, dividing the piano area from the art-filled living room.

168

Above: A.B. Clarke's house is a delight to behold. The seating area around the gridwork table is removed from the dragon screen in the background but remains under its spell. Japanese objets d'art chosen and arranged with exquisite care interact dynamically with comfortable, attractive furniture from the West and carpets from the Near East.

GRANDE DAME

Above: *The magnificent house built in 1925 by coal baron Gengo Matsuo combines the best of East and West. The graceful, European-style drawing room was originally two Japanese rooms. Modern Venetian glass chandeliers were carefully selected by Peter and Minchie Huggler, who have given much time and effort to preserving Japan's architectural past and sharing it with other people. The purely Japanese garden and exquisite Japanese wing behind are rare jewels in an old Tokyo that is fast vanishing.*

Left: *A Taisho-era, European-style sitting room overlooks a glorious Japanese garden.*

Right: Art from around the world is displayed in the dining-room gallery of Dr. and Mrs. Komei Okamoto. The eighteenth-century Spanish refectory table with mismatched Windsor chairs rests on a kilim rug, and an African chair is placed next to an autumn arrangement of maple branches by Harumi Nibe. The Okamotos constantly change the pieces in the third-floor gallery, always a source of wonder to both first-time visitors and old friends.

Below: A dramatic room in the ultramodern house of Hilary and Carlo Colombo. English and Italian, both have strong ideas about style. Contributing to this scene are Italian leather sofas, an Italian glass table, Korean pot lamps on kotatsu tables, and a checkerboard flower arrangement in red-lacquer boxes.

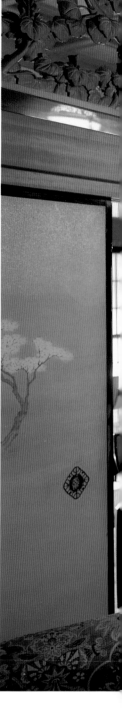

KYOTO IN TOKYO

This ideal of Japanese architecture was built in Kyoto at the turn of the century, when Japan was emerging from 250 years of isolation. Moved to Tokyo in 1963, the house combines the graceful elegance of traditional Japanese style with European furniture and carpets laid over tatami mats, creating a classic blend of East and West.

Above: Fusuma *can be used to divide rooms or create one large space. The skillful attention to architectural details can result in beauty anywhere, here in the beautifully carved* ranma *overhead.*

Right: The delicate painting was done on a lotus leaf, then framed and hung on a silk cord.

Opposite above: Shōji doors open to reveal unique black-lacquer door frames that open onto the inner garden. Two adjacent rooms divided by fusuma *are the ideal of European-style living within a Japanese aesthetic framework.*

Opposite below: Intricate details are found even on the sliding doors of a storage cupboard.

THE ART OF THE BATH

Of all the elements of the Japanese art of living, perhaps the ritual of the bath is the most widely imitated. Japanese bathrooms are treated as oases of peace and relaxation, designed to encourage lingering.

Above: The bathroom opens onto an inner garden with flowers, bamboo fence, and lantern. To retain heat, the wooden bathtub is covered when not in use.

Right: A guest bathroom amusingly employs an old wooden farm tool as a towel rack.

Opposite: The Kyoto hinoki (Japanese cypress) bathroom of Matt and Judy Forrest was specially installed to replace the original one. The buckets and stools, made of the much-prized hinoki, produce a distinctive fragrance. A crude vegetable basket covers the light, casting a diffused glow.

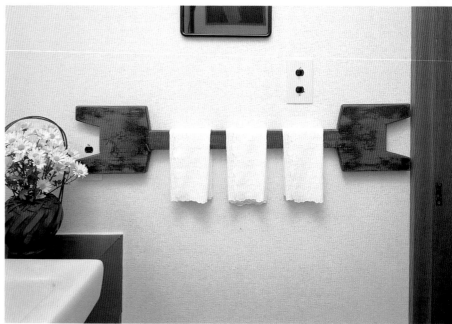

ART IN THE BATH

Left: The Japanese bath is a place for cleansing and purifying the body, and refreshing the spirit. Its importance as a place of rejuvenation and relaxation is paramount. Kida-san needs the deep, Japanese-style tub to soak his aching arms and shoulders after a day and night of carving wood blocks. The tranquillity of the wooden bath and the carefully chosen art objects refresh the spirit, while the hot water soothes the body.

Below: Antique blue and white Imari bathroom slippers were once used to straddle the conveniences in style. Today they are sometimes used for flower arrangements and sometimes left on the floor to remind people of the artistry that went into the making of the basic accoutrements of daily life.

Above left: *Vivid Italian stained-glass windows were specially ordered in the 1920s when this house was built. Decorated with Japanese themes, the windows make this bath not only a beautiful room but also a unique synthesis of East and West. Mt. Fuji is often painted on the walls of* sentō *(public baths).*

Above right: *A cutting from a piece of square bamboo makes an elegant and amusing soap dish.*

Left: *Stenciled* washi *covering the walls, a bamboo bench under the* sudare, *and a collection of folk toys make the Forrest guest bathroom a room worth visiting.*

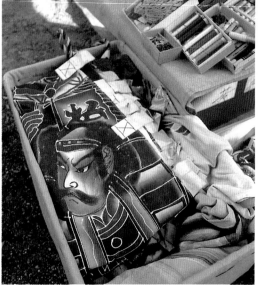

SOMETHING FOR EVERYONE

All the ingredients for living beautifully can be found at flea markets held weekly in Tokyo and monthly in Kyoto. The search is half the fun, as you wander through displays offering everything from teacups to an admiral's uniform.

Sources

There are many sources for the art of living in Japan. Department stores carry such huge selections of items that they can be overwhelming. Specialty shops are small and easier to deal with. Visiting antique shops can be useful too. Browsing through the pick of these shops is a good way to educate yourself before visiting the flea markets. On the following pages I have listed a number of my favorite shops and galleries where you can find most of the things shown in this book.

ANTIQUES

Antique Gallery Meguro
Stork Mansion, 2F
2-24-18 Kami Osaki, Shinagawa-ku
Tokyo 141 (03) 493-1971

Antique Market
Hanae Mori Bldg.
3-6-1 Kita Aoyama, Minato-ku
Tokyo 107 (03) 406-1021

Antiques Hasebeya
1-5-24 Azabu Juban, Minato-ku
Tokyo 106 (03) 401-9998

Bel Etage
AXIS Bldg., 2F
5-17-1 Roppongi, Minato-ku
Tokyo 106 (03) 587-0318

Gallery Ake
Hanae Mori Bldg., B1
3-6-1 Kita Aoyama, Minato-ku
Tokyo 107 (03) 407-4399

Gallery Hasebeya
3-11-3 Moto Azabu, Minato-ku
Tokyo 105 (03) 401-8840

Harumi Antiques
9-6-14 Akasaka, Minato-ku
Tokyo 107 (03) 403-1043

Honjo Gallery
Palace Aoyama
6-1-6 Minami Aoyama, Minato-ku
Tokyo 108 (03) 400-0277

House of Antiques
Yoshihiro Takishita
5-15-5 Kajiwara, Kamakura
Kanagawa Prefecture 247
(0467) 43-1441
FAX (0467) 45-8245

Kathryn Milan
3-1-14 Nishi Azabu, Minato-ku
Tokyo 106 (03) 408-1532

Kikori
Hanae Mori Bldg., B1
3-6-1 Kita Aoyama, Minato-ku
Tokyo 107 (03) 407-9363

Kurofune, John Adair
7-7-4 Roppongi, Minato-ku
Tokyo 106 (03) 479-1552

Magatani Co., Ltd.
5-10-13 Toranomon, Minato-ku
Tokyo 105 (03) 433-6321

Morita Antiques
5-12-2 Minami Aoyama, Minato-ku
Tokyo 107 (03) 407-4466

Nakamura Antiques
2-24-9 Nishi Azabu, Minato-ku
Tokyo 106 (03) 486-0636

Okura Oriental Art
Kenji Tsuchisawa
3-3-14 Azabudai, Minato-ku
Tokyo 106 (03) 585-5309

Oriental Bazaar
5-9-13 Jingumae, Shibuya-ku
Tokyo 150 (03) 400-3933

Yokohama Sogo Department Store
Japan Shop, 6F, Yokohama Station
2-18-1 Takashima, Nishi-ku
Yokohama, Kanagawa Prefecture 220
(045) 465-2111 Ext. 5686

BASKETS

Harumi Antiques
9-6-14 Akasaka, Minato-ku
Tokyo 107 (03) 403-1043

NOTE: Telephone numbers in Tokyo now have four-digit prefixes. To numbers with three-digit prefixes, add a 3 at the start of the prefix.

Kathryn Milan
3-1-14 Nishi Azabu, Minato-ku
Tokyo 106 (03) 408-1532

Kurofune, John Adair
7-7-4 Roppongi, Minato-ku
Tokyo 106 (03) 479-1552

Morita Antiques
5-12-2 Minami Aoyama, Minato-ku
Tokyo 107 (03) 407-4466

Okura Oriental Art
3-3-14 Azabudai, Minato-ku
Tokyo 106 (03) 585-5309

CERAMICS AND PORCELAIN

Antiques Nishikawa
2-20-14 Azabu Juban, Minato-ku
Tokyo 106 (03) 456-1023

Savoir Vivre
AXIS Bldg.
5-17-1 Roppongi, Minato-ku
Tokyo 106 (03) 585-7365

Yokohama Sogo Department Store
2-18-1 Takashima, Nishi-ku
Yokohama, Kanagawa Prefecture 220
(045) 465-2111

Yokohama Takashimaya
Yokohama Station
1-6-31 Minami Saiwai, Nishi-ku
Yokohama, Kanagawa Prefecture 220
(045) 311-5111

Yoshicho Mentels
1-11-4 Nishi Azabu, Minato-ku
Tokyo 106 (03) 402-9480

CONTEMPORARY CRAFTS

Craft Space Wa
2-11-12 Shibuya, Shibuya-ku
Tokyo 150 (03) 797-3567

Japan Folk Craft Museum
(Nihon Mingeikan)
4-3-33 Komaba, Meguro-ku
Tokyo 153 (03) 467-4527

Japan Traditional Craft Center
Plaza 246 Bldg., 2F
3-1-1 Minami Aoyama, Minato-ku
Tokyo 107 (03) 403-2460

Kisso
AXIS Bldg.
5-17-1 Roppongi, Minato-ku
Tokyo 106 (03) 582-4191

Maruzen
Crafts Gallery, 4F
2-3-10 Nihonbashi, Chuo-ku
Tokyo 103 (03) 272-7211

Matsuya Department Store
Crafts Gallery
3-6-1 Ginza, Chuo-ku
Tokyo 104 (03) 567-1211

LACQUERWARE

Heiando
3-10-11 Nihonbashi, Chuo-ku
Tokyo 103 (03) 272-2871

Japan Traditional Craft Center
Plaza 246 Bldg., 2F
3-1-1 Minami Aoyama, Minato-ku
Tokyo 107 (03) 403-2460

Twos
3-17-14 Minami Azabu, Minato-ku
Tokyo 106 (03) 440-2384

MINGEI

Beniya
2-16-8 Shibuya, Shibuya-ku
Tokyo 150 (03) 400-8084

Bingoya
10-6 Wakamatsu-cho, Shinjuku-ku
Tokyo 162 (03) 202-8778

Folk Craft Shop Ebine
New Gaien Heights
4-5-1 Sendagaya, Shibuya-ku
Tokyo 151 (03) 408-9380

Japan Folk Craft Museum
(Nihon Mingeikan)

4-3-33 Komaba, Meguro-ku
Tokyo 153 (03) 467-4527

Takumi
8-4-2 Ginza, Chuo-ku
Tokyo 104 (03) 571-2017

PRINTS

Franell Gallery
Hotel Okura
2-10-4 Toranomon, Minato-ku
Tokyo 105 (03) 583-2751

Tolman Collection
2-2-18 Shiba Daimon, Minato-ku
Tokyo 105 (03) 434-1300

Yoseido Gallery
5-5-15 Ginza, Chuo-ku
Tokyo 104 (03) 571-1312

SCREENS, SCROLLS, AND ART

Designer Screens, Maureen Duxbury
1-10-19 Hatanodai, Shinagawa-ku
Tokyo 142 (03) 787-9860

Eastgate Antiques
(screens for purchase or lease)
3-27-7 Nozawa, Setagaya-ku
Tokyo 154 (03) 414-6601

Harumi Antiques
9-6-14 Akasaka, Minato-ku
Tokyo 107 (03) 403-1043

Heisando
1-2-4 Shiba Koen, Minato-ku
Tokyo 107 (03) 343-0588

House of Antiques
5-15-5 Kajiwara, Kamakura
Kanagawa Prefecture 247
(0467) 43-1441

Kathryn Milan
3-1-14 Nishi Azabu, Minato-ku
Tokyo 106 (03) 408-1532

Suzuki Screen
(sales, repair, and remounting)

3-23-1 Hatchobori, Chuo-ku
Tokyo 104 (03) 551-5827

TEXTILES (Kyoto)

Aizen Kobo
Nakasuji-dori, Omiya, Nishi-iru
Kamikyo-ku, Kyoto 602
(075) 441-0355

Konjaku Nishimura
381 Moto-cho
Yamato-oji, Higashi-iru
Furumonzen-dori
Higashiyama-ku, Kyoto 605
(075) 561-1312
            (and)
Nawate-dori, Furumonzen Sagaru
Higashiyama-ku, Kyoto 605
(075) 561-1568

Mitsuno
367-1 Moto-cho
Yamato-oji, Higashi-iru
Furumonzen-dori
Higashiyama-ku, Kyoto 605
(075) 531-0241

Mizutani Yoko
227-2 Nishi-no-cho
Nawate Higashi-iru
Shinmonzen-dori
Higashiyama-ku, Kyoto 605
(075) 561-5711

Nakamura Chingire-ten
Sanjo Minami-iru, Nawate-dori
Higashiyama-ku, Kyoto 605
(075) 561-4726

TEXTILES (Tokyo)

Akariya 1
4-8-1 Yoyogi, Shibuya-ku
Tokyo 151 (03) 465-5578

Akariya 2
KS Bldg.
5-58-1 Yoyogi, Shibuya-ku
Tokyo 151 (03) 467-0580

Antique Gallery Meguro
Stork Mansion, 2F
2-24-18 Kami Osaki, Shinagawa-ku
Tokyo 141 (03) 493-1971

Gallery Ake
Hanae Mori Bldg., B1
3-6-1 Kita Aoyama, Minato-ku
Tokyo 107 (03) 407-4399

Harumi Antiques
9-6-14 Akasaka, Minato-ku
Tokyo 107 (03) 403-1043

Hayashi Kimono
International Arcade
1-7-23 Uchisaiwaicho, Chiyoda-ku
Tokyo 100 (03) 591-9825

Ikeda, Antique Textiles
101 Softtown Shirogane
5-22-11 Shiroganedai, Minato-ku
Tokyo 108 (03) 445-1269

Morita Antiques
5-12-2 Minami Aoyama, Minato-ku
Tokyo 107 (03) 407-4466

Nuno
AXIS Bldg., B1
5-17-1 Roppongi, Minato-ku
Tokyo 106 (03) 582-7997

Sei
Hanae Mori Bldg., basement
3-6-1 Kita Aoyama, Minato-ku
Tokyo 107 (03) 407-7541

Teoriya
Ogi Bldg., 2F
2-8 Ogawamachi, Kanda, Chiyoda-ku
Tokyo 101 (03) 294-3903

WASHI PAPER

Isetatsu
2-18-9 Yanaka, Taito-ku
Tokyo 110 (03) 823-1453

Itoya
2-7-15 Ginza, Chuo-ku
Tokyo 104 (03) 561-8311

Otsu Washi
Otsu Bldg., basement
2-6-3 Honcho, Nihonbashi, Chuo-ku
Tokyo 103 (03) 663-8788

Paper Nao
KS Sengoku Bldg.
1-29-12-201 Sengoku, Bunkyo-ku
Tokyo 112 (03) 944-4470

Sakura Horikiri
1-26-2 Yanagibashi, Taito-ku
Tokyo 111 (03) 863-6600

Suzando Hashimoto
Fuya-cho, Higashi-iru
Rokkaku-dori
Nakagyo-ku, Kyoto 604
(075) 223-0347
        (and)
New Melsa, 6F
5-7-12 Ginza, Chuo-ku
Tokyo 104 (03) 573-1497
        (and)
Tokyu Plaza, 4F
1-2-2 Dogenzaka, Shibuya-ku
Tokyo 150 (03) 463-3437

Washikobo
1-8-10 Nishi Azabu, Minato-ku
Tokyo 106 (03) 405-1841

TOKYO SHOPS WITH JAPANACHE
Galleries and Shops

Blue & White
2-9-2 Azabu Juban, Minato-ku
Tokyo 106 (03) 451-0537

Boutique Yuya
3-6-4 Nishi Azabu, Minato-ku
Tokyo 106 (03) 5474-2097

Comme des Garçons
5-2-1 Minami Aoyama, Minato-ku
Tokyo 107 (03) 406-3951

Gallery Ikat
4-12-8-103 Jingumae, Shibuya-ku
Tokyo 150 (03) 403-0820

Issey Miyake
From 1st
5-3-10 Minami Aoyama, Minato-ku
Tokyo 107 (03) 499-6476

Nuno
AXIS Bldg., B1
5-17-1 Roppongi, Minato-ku
Tokyo 106 (03) 582-7997

Plantation
Issey Miyake Permanente
Tessen Bldg., B1, 1F
4-21-29 Minami Aoyama, Minato-ku
Tokyo 107 (03) 423-1408 Plantation
         (03) 470-7488 Permanente

Sagacho Space
Shokuryo Bldg., 3F
1-8-13 Saga, Koto-ku
Tokyo 135 (03) 630-3243

Savior Vivre Gallery
AXIS Bldg., 3F
5-17-1 Roppongi, Minato-ku
Tokyo 106 (03) 587-1898

Spiral Bldg. Market
(exhibits and Sunday brunch in lobby)
5-6-23 Minami Aoyama, Minato-ku
Tokyo 107 (03) 498-1171

Restaurants

Atagoya
6-13-12 Shimbashi, Minato-ku
Tokyo 105 (03) 578-1279

Bon
1-2-11 Ryusen, Taito-ku
Tokyo 110 (03) 872-0375

Goemon
1-1-26 Hon Komagome, Bunkyo-ku
Tokyo 113 (03) 811-2015
         (03) 812-0900

Hikage Jaya
Ishimaru Bldg., B1
5-2-35 Minami Azabu, Minato-ku
Tokyo 106 (03) 473-0014

Ichioku
4-4-5 Roppongi, Minato-ku
Tokyo 106 (03) 405-9891

Kamikaze
5-8-5 Jingumae, Shibuya-ku
Tokyo 150 (03) 498-1682

Kihachi
4-18-10 Minami Aoyama, Minato-ku
Tokyo 107 (03) 403-7477

Kiku
4-26-27 Jingumae, Shibuya-ku
Tokyo 150 (03) 408-4919

Kisso
AXIS Bldg., B1
5-17-1 Roppongi, Minato-ku
Tokyo 106 (03) 582-4704
         (03) 582-4191

Kuremutsu
2-2-13 Asakusa, Taito-ku
Tokyo 111 (03) 842-0906

Matsumoto
Garden Plaza Hiro, 2F
4-1-29 Minami Azabu, Minato-ku
Tokyo 106 (03) 442-7647

Tatsumiya
1-33-5 Asakusa, Taito-ku
Tokyo 111 (03) 842-7373

Tonki
1-1-2 Shimo Meguro, Meguro-ku
Tokyo 153 (03) 491-9928

MUSEUMS

*NOTE: Most museums in Japan are closed
on Monday.*

Hara Museum
4-7-25 Kita Shinagawa, Shinagawa-ku
Tokyo 140 (03) 445-0651

Hara Museum ARK
Kanai 2844
Shibukawa, Gumma Prefecture 377
(0279) 24-6585

Hatakeyama Museum
2-20-12 Shiroganedai, Minato-ku
Tokyo 108 (03) 447-5787

Idemitsu Art Gallery
3-1-1 Marunouchi, Chiyoda-ku
Tokyo 100 (03) 213-9402

Japanese Museum of Traditional Houses
7-1-1 Masukata, Tama-ku
Kawasaki, Kanagawa Prefecture 230
(044) 922-2181

Japan Folk Craft Museum
4-3-33 Komaba, Meguro-ku
Tokyo 153 (03) 467-4527

Kitakamakura Textile Museum
Ofuna 2135
Kamakura, Kanagawa Prefecture 247
(0467) 43-4141

Kyoto National Museum
527 Chayamachi, Higashiyama-ku
Kyoto 605 (075) 541-1151

MOA Museum of Art
26-2 Momoyama-cho
Atami, Shizuoka Prefecture 413
(0557) 84-2500

Nara National Museum
50 Noboriojicho
Nara, Nara Prefecture 630
(0742) 22-7771

National Museum of Modern Art,
  Tokyo (Crafts Gallery)
1-1 Kitanomaru Koen, Chiyoda-ku
Tokyo 102 (03) 211-7781

Nezu Art Museum
6-5-36 Minami Aoyama, Minato-ku
Tokyo 107 (03) 400-2536

Suntory Art Gallery
Tokyo Suntory Bldg., 11F
1-2-3 Moto Akasaka, Minato-ku
Tokyo 107 (03) 470-1073

Tokyo National Museum
8-36 Ueno Park, Taito-ku
Tokyo 110 (03) 823-6921

Yuasa Museum
International Christian University
30-10-2 Osawa
Mitaka, Tokyo 181 (0422) 33-3340

JAPANACHE IN THE UNITED STATES
Shops, Museums, and Galleries

HONOLULU

Honolulu Academy of Arts
900 South Beretania Street
Honolulu, HI 96814

ILLINOIS

Art Institute of Chicago
Michigan Avenue and Adams Street
Chicago, IL 60603

KANSAS

Spencer Museum of Art
University of Kansas
Lawrence, KS 66045

LOS ANGELES

Konishi Gallery
5905 Wilshire Boulevard
Los Angeles, CA 90036

Los Angeles County Museum of Art
5905 Wilshire Boulevard
Los Angeles, CA 90036

Pacific Asia Museum
46 North Los Robles Avenue
Pasadena, CA 91101

MASSACHUSETTS

Boston Children's Museum
300 Congress Street
Boston, MA 02110

Museum of Fine Arts
465 Huntington Avenue
Boston, MA 02115

Peabody Museum of Salem
East India Square
Salem, MA 01970

MISSOURI

Asiatica Ltd.
205 Westport Road
Kansas City, MO 64111

Nelson-Atkins Museum of Art
4525 Oak Street
Kansas City, MO 64111

NEW YORK Galleries and Shops

Art Asia
1086 Madison Avenue
New York, NY 10028

Asian Rare Book, Inc.
234 Fifth Avenue, 3F
New York, NY 10001

Brooklyn Museum Gift Shop
200 Eastern Parkway
Brooklyn, NY 11238

Naga Antiques Ltd.
145 East 61st Street
New York, NY 10021

Paragon Books
237 West 72nd Street
New York, NY 10023

Sugimoto Works of Art
398 West Broadway
New York, NY 10012

NEW YORK Museums

Asia Society
Rockefeller Collection
112 East 64th Street
New York, NY 10021

Brooklyn Museum
200 Eastern Parkway
Brooklyn, NY 11238

Isamu Noguchi Museum
32-27 Vernon Boulevard
Long Island City, NY 11106

Japan Society
Japan House Gallery
333 East 47th Street
New York, NY 10017

Metropolitan Museum of Art
Sackler Wing
Fifth Avenue at 82nd Street
New York, NY 10028

SAN FRANCISCO

Crane & the Turtle
2550 California Street
San Francisco, CA 94115

Japonesque
Crocker Center Gallery 54
50 Post Street
San Francisco, CA 94104

Kasuri Dyeworks
1959 Shattuck Avenue
Berkeley, CA 94704

Kuromatsu Gallery
722 Bay Street
San Francisco, CA 94109

Museum of Asian Art
Golden Gate Park
San Francisco, CA 94118

SEATTLE

Crane Gallery
12038 Second Avenue
Seattle, WA 98101

Seattle Art Museum
Volunteer Park
Seattle, WA 98112

TEXAS

Kimbell Museum of Art
3333 Camp Bowie Boulevard
Fort Worth, TX 76107

WASHINGTON, D.C.

Arthur M. Sackler Gallery
Smithsonian Institution
Independence Avenue at 11th Street SW
Washington, D.C. 20560

Freer Gallery
Smithsonian Institution
Jefferson Drive at 12th Street SW
Washington, D.C. 20560

Nomi no ichi (flea markets) proliferate in Tokyo and throughout Japan. Finding the best markets and attending them regularly can make for family outings that are fun and educational. With the exception of the Heiwajima Antiques Fair and the market at the Roi building in Roppongi, flea markets are held outdoors and canceled in case of rain. Most markets start at sunrise (though addicts have been known to shop by flashlight!) and continue until four or five in the afternoon. Dates and location changes are regularly printed in newspapers, shopping guides, tourist magazines, and other publications. The following are some of Japan's best-known flea markets:

First Sunday of the month
Arai Yakushi Temple
Arai Yakushijimae Station
on the Seibu Shinjuku Line

First and fourth Sundays
Togo Shrine
Harajuku Station
on the Yamanote Line
  (or)
Meiji Jingumae Station
on the Chiyoda Line

Second Sunday
Nogi Shrine
Nogizaka Station
on the Chiyoda Line

Second and third Sundays
Hanazono Shrine
Shinjuku-san-chome Station
on the Marunouchi Line

Fourth Thursday and Friday
Roi Bldg.
Roppongi Station
on the Hibiya Line

21st of the month
Toji Shrine
Kyoto

25th of the month
Kitano Shrine
Kyoto

28th of the month
Narita Fudo Shrine
Kawagoe, Saitama Prefecture
on the Tobu Tojo Line

December 15, 16
  (and)
January 15, 16
Boro Ichi
Setagaya Station
on the Setagaya Line

March, June, September, December
Heiwajima Antiques Fair
Ryutsu Center Station
on the Tokyo Monorail
from Hamamatsucho Station
on the Yamanote Line

Bibliography

Adachi, Barbara. *The Living Treasures of Japan*. Tokyo, New York, San Francisco: Kodansha International Ltd., 1973.

Brandon, Reiko Mochinaga. *Country Textiles of Japan*. New York, Tokyo: Weatherhill, 1986.

Durston, Diane. *Old Kyoto*. Tokyo, New York, San Francisco: Kodansha International Ltd., 1987.

Grilli, Elise. *The Art of the Japanese Screen*. New York, Tokyo: Weatherhill, Bijutsu-sha, 1987.

Hauge, Victor, and Takako Hauge. *Folk Traditions in Japanese Art*. New York, Tokyo: Weatherhill, 1973.

Havens, Thomas R.H. *Artist and Patron in Postwar Japan*. Princeton, NJ: Princeton University Press, 1982.

Hibi, Sadao, ed. *Japanese Tradition in Color and Form*. Tokyo: Graphic-sha Publication Co., Ltd., 1987.

Hirai, Noriko. *Tsutsugaki Textiles of Japan*. Kyoto: Shikosha, 1987.

Kawashima, Chuji. *Design of Japanese Folk Houses*. Tokyo: Sagami Shobo, 1986.

Kawashima, Chuji. *Minka: Traditional Houses of Rural Japan*. Tokyo, New York, San Francisco: Kodansha International Ltd., 1986.

Kojima, Setsuko, and Gene A. Crane. *A Dictionary of Japanese Culture*. Tokyo: Japan Times, 1987.

Koren, Leonard. *New Fashion Japan*. Tokyo, New York, San Francisco: Kodansha International Ltd., 1984.

Lee, Sherman. *Japanese Decorative Style*. Cleveland: Cleveland Museum of Art, 1961.

Lee, Sherman. *The Genius of Japanese Design*. Tokyo, New York, San Francisco: Kodansha International Ltd., 1981.

Massy, Patricia. *Sketches of Japanese Crafts*. Tokyo: Japan Times, 1980.

Minnich, Helen Benton. *Japanese Costume*. Tokyo and Rutland, Vermont: Charles E. Tuttle Company, 1963.

Morse, Edward Sylvester. *Japanese Homes and Their Surroundings*. Kyoto: Kyoto Shoin Company Ltd., 1988.

Nibe, Harumi. *Hyaku no Midori no Naka de*. Tokyo: Bunka Shuppan, 1987.

Okakura, Kakuzo. *The Book of Tea*. Tokyo and Rutland, Vermont: Charles E. Tuttle Company, 1956.

Salmon, Patricia. *Japanese Antiques*. Tokyo: Art International Publishers, 1975.

Shirasu, Masako. *Hana*. Tokyo: Shimmu Shoko, 1989.

Slesin, Suzanne, et. al. *Japanese Style*. New York: Clarkson N. Potter Inc., 1987.

Statler, Oliver. *Japanese Inn*. New York: Random House, 1961.

Stern, Harold P. *Birds, Beasts, Blossoms, and Bugs: The Nature of Japan*. New York: Harry N. Abrams Inc., 1976.

Sudo, Isao. *Nihon Seikatsu Jibiki*. Tokyo: Kobundon, 1989.

Tanaka, Ikko, et. al. *Japan Design*. Tokyo: Libro Port Company, Ltd., 1984.

Tanaka, Ikko, et. al. *Japanese Coloring*. Tokyo: Libro Port Company, Ltd., 1984.

Tanizaki, Junichiro. *In Praise of Shadows*. Tokyo and Rutland, Vermont: Charles E. Tuttle Company, 1984.

Tsubouchi, Fujio. *Akari no Kodogu*. Tokyo: Kogei Shuppan, 1987.

Watson, William, ed. *The Great Japan Exhibition, Art of the Edo Period, 1600–1868*. London: Royal Academy of Arts, 1981–82.

Yagi, Koji. *A Japanese Touch for Your Home*. Tokyo, New York, San Francisco: Kodansha International Ltd., 1982.

Yanagi, Soetsu. *Folk Crafts in Japan*. Tokyo: Kokusai Bunka Shinkokai, 1949.

Yoshida, Mitsukuni, et. al. *Japan Style*. Tokyo, New York, San Francisco: Kodansha International Ltd., 1980.

Glossary-Index

Italicized numbers indicate pages containing definitions or other information in text; roman numbers indicate pages with photographs.